Adobe® Photoshop® CS5

Level 1

Adobe® Photoshop® CS5: Level 1

Part Number: 084384
Course Edition: 1.0

NOTICES

HELP US IMPROVE OUR COURSEWARE

Your comments are important to us. Please contact us at Element K Press LLC, 1-800-478-7788, 500 Canal View Boulevard, Rochester, NY 14623, Attention: Product Planning, or through our Web site at **http://support.elementkcourseware.com**.

Adobe® Photoshop® CS5: Level 1

About This Course

As an aspiring graphic designer, you would like to familiarize yourself with design creation and image editing using Adobe® Photoshop® CS5. Understanding the different tools and features available in Photoshop CS5 will help you maximize your creative potential. In this course, you will use the various tools and features of Photoshop CS5 to work with images.

Photoshop CS5 has a user-friendly interface with a variety of tools and features to help you design, create, and enhance images, and produce professional designs for both print and web.

Course Description

Target Student

Adobe® Photoshop® CS5: Level 1 is intended for a diverse audience including, but not limited to, computer-savvy professionals who want to create and enhance graphics for marketing materials, newsletters, blogs, and websites; photographers who want to work with and prepare photos for print or web; students with an interest in graphic design or those with novice design skills; and professionals who want to learn and use Photoshop CS5 as a complement to other CS5 programs, such as Illustrator. The course covers the Adobe Visual Communication using Photoshop CS5 objectives, and is intended to help prepare students to take the Adobe Certified Associate exam. Please refer to the CD-ROM that came with this course for a document that maps the Adobe Visual Communication using Photoshop CS5 objectives to the content in the Adobe Photoshop CS5 series.

Course Prerequisites

Before taking this course, students should be familiar with the basic functions of their computer's operating system such as creating folders, launching programs, and working with windows. Students should also have basic Windows application skills, such as copying and pasting objects, formatting text, saving files, and so on.

Course Objectives

In this course, you will understand and use the various elements in the Photoshop CS5 interface so as to efficiently work with the software. You will use the different tools in Photoshop for selecting parts of images and identify the need for having layers in a Photoshop document. You will also organize the different components of the design as layers. With the layered Photoshop document thus created, you will apply layer effects and other special effects in order to enhance the appearance of the design. Once the design is finalized, you will save images in both print and web formats.

You will:

- Initiate a project.

- Explore the Adobe Photoshop CS5 environment.

- Determine the resolution and graphic type.

- Work with selections.

- Work with multiple layers.

- Enhance images with paint and filters.

- Identify the characteristics of various image modes and color adjustment options.

- Save images for web and print.

- Manage assets by using the various tools in Adobe® Bridge. This will enable you to organize your files and work more efficiently.

How to Use This Book

As a Learning Guide

This book is divided into lessons and topics, covering a subject or a set of related subjects. In most cases, lessons are arranged in order of increasing proficiency.

The results-oriented topics include relevant and supporting information you need to master the content. Each topic has various types of activities designed to enable you to practice the guidelines and procedures as well as to solidify your understanding of the informational material presented in the course.

At the back of the book, you will find a glossary of the definitions of the terms and concepts used throughout the course. You will also find an index to assist in locating information within the instructional components of the book.

In the Classroom

This book is intended to enhance and support the in-class experience. Procedures and guidelines are presented in a concise fashion along with activities and discussions. Information is provided for reference and reflection in such a way as to facilitate understanding and practice.

Each lesson may also include a Lesson Lab or various types of simulated activities. You will find the files for the simulated activities along with the other course files on the enclosed CD-ROM. If your course manual did not come with a CD-ROM, please go to **http://elementkcourseware.com** to download the files. If included, these interactive activities enable you to practice your skills in an immersive business environment, or to use hardware and software resources not available in the classroom. The course files that are available on the CD-ROM or by download may also contain sample files, support files, and additional reference materials for use both during and after the course.

As a Teaching Guide

Effective presentation of the information and skills contained in this book requires adequate preparation. As such, as an instructor, you should familiarize yourself with the content of the entire course, including its organization and approaches. You should review each of the student activities and exercises so you can facilitate them in the classroom.

Throughout the book, you may see Instructor Notes that provide suggestions, answers to problems, and supplemental information for you, the instructor. You may also see references to "Additional Instructor Notes" that contain expanded instructional information; these notes appear in a separate section at the back of the book. PowerPoint slides may be provided on the included course files, which are available on the enclosed CD-ROM or by download from http://elementkcourseware.com. The slides are also referred to in the text. If you plan to use the slides, it is recommended to display them during the corresponding content as indicated in the instructor notes in the margin.

The course files may also include assessments for the course, which can be administered diagnostically before the class, or as a review after the course is completed. These exam-type questions can be used to gauge the students' understanding and assimilation of course content.

As a Review Tool

Any method of instruction is only as effective as the time and effort you, the student, are willing to invest in it. In addition, some of the information that you learn in class may not be important to you immediately, but it may become important later. For this reason, we encourage you to spend some time reviewing the content of the course after your time in the classroom.

As a Reference

The organization and layout of this book make it an easy-to-use resource for future reference. Taking advantage of the glossary, index, and table of contents, you can use this book as a first source of definitions, background information, and summaries.

Course Icons

Icon	Description
	A **Caution Note** makes students aware of potential negative consequences of an action, setting, or decision that are not easily known.
	Display Slide provides a prompt to the instructor to display a specific slide. Display Slides are included in the Instructor Guide only.
	An **Instructor Note** is a comment to the instructor regarding delivery, classroom strategy, classroom tools, exceptions, and other special considerations. Instructor Notes are included in the Instructor Guide only.
	Notes Page indicates a page that has been left intentionally blank for students to write on.
	A **Student Note** provides additional information, guidance, or hints about a topic or task.
	A **Version Note** indicates information necessary for a specific version of software.

Course Requirements

Hardware

- Intel® Pentium® 4, Intel® Centrino®, Intel® Xeon®, or Intel® Core™ Duo (or compatible) processor
- 1GB RAM or above
- 1GB hard-disk space to install software and an additional 500 MB to run the course
- Color monitor with 16-bit or greater video card; 24-bit color recommended
- A mouse or compatible tracking device
- 1024 x 768 or higher monitor resolution
- CD-ROM drive
- A display system to project the instructor's computer screen

Software

- Microsoft® Windows® XP with Service Pack 3
- Adobe® Photoshop® CS5
- Adobe® Acrobat® Reader® 7.0 or above

Class Setup

1. Install Windows XP Professional on the C drive using the following parameters:
   a. Accept the license agreement.
   b. Create a 4 GB partition on the C drive.
   c. Format the C partition to NTFS.
   d. Select the appropriate regional and language settings.

  e. Enter the appropriate name and organization for your environment.

  f. Enter the product key.

  g. For each student computer, configure the settings:

   ■ Name of computer: **Computer#** (where # is a unique integer representing the student computer)

   ■ Administrator password: **password**

   ■ Select your time zone

   ■ Select the **Typical** network configuration

2. On the course CD-ROM, run the 084384.exe self-extracting file located within. This will install a folder named 084384a on your C drive. This folder contains all the data files that you will use to complete this course. Solution files are also provided in this folder. These files may help you find a possible solution if you get stuck at any point during the course. If you would like to view the final output or solution of an activity, navigate to the respective lesson\solution folder.

3. Perform a complete installation of Adobe Acrobat Reader 7.0 or above.

4. In order to ensure that all features of Photoshop will be available for this course, run a standard installation from the software installation CD.

  a. Run the **setup.exe** file.

  b. In the **Adobe Photoshop CS5: License Agreement** window, click **ACCEPT.**

  c. In the **Adobe Photoshop CS5: Serial Number** window, enter the serial key.

  d. In the **Adobe Photoshop CS5:** window, from the **Select Language** drop-down list, select **English (North America)** and click **Next.**

  e. In the **Adobe Photoshop CS5: Install Options** window, click **Install.**

  f. In the **Adobe Photoshop CS5: Installation Progress** window, click **Finish.**

  g. In the **Adobe Photoshop CS5: Installation Progress** window, verify that the "100% Complete" message is displayed and click **DONE.**

5. It is recommend that your monitor resolution be set to at least 1024 x 768 for optimal performance.

6. In addition to the specific setup procedures needed for this class to run properly, you should also check the Element K Press product support website at http://support.elementkcourseware.com for more information. Any updates about this course will be posted there.

Install Optional Plug-ins

1. Download the Photoshop **PHSPCS4_Optional_Plug-Ins.zip** file from the http://www.adobe.com/support/downloads/detail.jsp?ftpID=4048 site.

2. Unzip the **PHSPCS4_Optional_Plug-Ins.zip** file.

3. Double-click the **PHSPCS4_Cont_LS1.exe** file.

4. In the **Adobe Photoshop CS4 Content** dialog box, specify the location where you want to save the files.

5. In the location where you have saved the file, double-click the **English** folder and navigate to **Goodies\Optional plug-ins\Plug-ins 32–bit\Automate** folder.

6. Select all the files and copy them.

7. Navigate to the C:\Program Files\Adobe\Adobe Photoshop CS5\Plug-ins\Automate folder and paste the copied files.

8. Similarly, navigate to the Goodies\Presets folder. Copy the Layouts folder.

9. Navigate to C:\Program Files\Adobe\Adobe Photoshop CS5\Presets folder and paste the Layouts folder.

Install the Decorative Fonts

1. Navigate to the C:\084384Data\Fonts folder and copy the fonts.

2. Choose **Start→Control Panel.**

3. In the left pane, click **Classic View.**

4. Open the Fonts folder and paste the copied font.

List of Additional Files

Printed with each activity is a list of files students open to complete that activity. Many activities also require additional files that students do not open, but are needed to support the file(s) students are working with. These supporting files are included with the student data files on the course CD-ROM or data disk. Do not delete these files.

1 Initiating a Project

Lesson Time: 20 minutes

Lesson Objectives:

In this lesson, you will initiate a project.

You will:

- Examine the elements of a well-designed project plan.
- Identify copyright and citation requirements.

Introduction

Before familiarizing yourself with Photoshop, you need to know how a project is initiated and executed and what factors will influence the development of a project. Planning is one of the primary keys in developing projects efficiently. In this lesson, you will plan a project to ensure that the project meets specific objectives and to streamline the development process.

Planning forms an integral part of everybody's life. While some make huge plans for birthdays, some plan for higher studies, weddings, or parties. All these events commence with a plan outlay where each single and integral aspect is noted and worked out to its execution. The decisions made during this phase ensure smooth flow of other phases associated with it. A well-thought-out and well-designed project plan ensures that the project is successful throughout, from initiation to delivery.

This lesson covers all or part of the following Adobe Visual Communication using Photoshop CS5 objectives:

- Topic A
  - Objective 1.1a: Identify information that determines purpose, audience, and audience needs for image production.
  - Objective 1.3a: Identify items that might appear on a project plan.
  - Objective 1.3b: Identify phases that might appear on a project plan.
  - Objective 1.3c: Identify deliverables that might be produced during the project.
  - Objective 1.3d: Identify common problems and issues in project management.
  - Objective 1.4: Communicate with others (such as peers and clients) about design plans.
- Topic B

- ■ Objective 1.2a: Use copyright terms correctly, such as copyrighted, fair use doctrine, intellectual property, and derivative works.

- ■ Objective 1.2b: Identify when permission must be obtained to use copyrighted material.

- ■ Objective 1.2c: Identify methods used to indicate that images are copyrighted.

TOPIC A
Plan a Project

You have made an attempt to use Adobe Photoshop to work with editing images. Before you start working on projects, you need to plan how to develop a project. In this topic, you will plan a project to ensure that it covers the required parameters and meets the objectives.

When planning a Photoshop project, it is important that you spend time understanding the project's requirements and specifications. A well-planned project ensures that you are confident about the assets you use, the actions you want to perform, the overall environment, the design considerations, the design layout, the final output, and the end user. With effective planning, you can make a project successful, spending less time and resources on development and design.

Projects

Definition:

A *project* is a temporary undertaking with a clearly defined beginning and ending that results in a unique product or service. It is different from an organization's ongoing operations because mostly, a project ends when its objectives are achieved. Projects lend themselves to a teamwork structure because they draw from a range of disciplines to complete the work. Projects can vary widely in terms of the budget, staff size, duration, expected outcome, and end user.

Example:

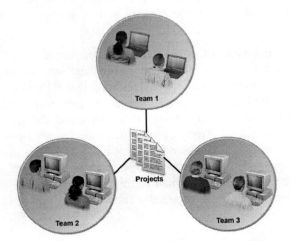

Figure 1-1: Projects drawing input from various teams and disciplines to meet the objectives.

Project Plan Phases

Project phases are often referred to as the project life cycle that covers a project from project evaluation to planning, project execution to launch. Projects are typically broken down into manageable, sequential phases—each with its own definitions and deliverables. For example, a project process might begin by defining the audience and goals, followed by setting up the project structure. Once the structure is built, the execution process begins. After the project plan has been reviewed and approved, the project moves into the build and testing phase. After the testing phase, the project deliverables are ready for launch.

Items Appearing In a Project Plan

When managing the design and development of, say a software project, such as Photoshop, your plan might contain the design elements, image specifications, technology to be used, resources, final output, target audience, and various other factors.

Project Plan Deliverables

A project deliverable is an output from a project management activity that is measurable, unique, and verifiable. During the phases of the project life cycle, successive layers of detail are added to the project plan as the project progresses. This sequence of phases usually involves a handoff or a deliverable. The deliverables from one phase of a project serve as inputs to the subsequent phase. Project deliverables require the approval and sign-off of the project stakeholders.

Supporting Plans

A project plan is usually supported by other plans that detail individual components of a project plan. Commonly used supporting plans are resource plans that identify the resources available and describe their roles and responsibilities, communication plans that identify communication methods, risk management plans that detail actions to be taken when unexpected events occur, quality plans, budget, and procurement plans, scope, delivery schedules, and other related plans.

Communication plans are an important component of most projects. To ensure smooth progress of a project, extensive communication is required among team members, stakeholders, and clients. Team members need to be informed about decisions that will affect the development of a project. Communication with clients at regular intervals is required to keep them informed about the progress of the project and any change that will affect the final outcome of the project. In addition to establishing a strong communication channel between the client and the project team, it is also important to consider factors such as resource planning and risk management. Resource planning and backup must ensure that resources are available throughout to execute the project plan deliverables. Risk management factors include plans for foreseeing risks and planning for them in advance, especially those arising out of infrastructure, resources, cost, time, and so on.

Scope

Scope refers to the range, breadth, and parameters of the work assignment. A scope statement defines what the project is and what it does and does not need to accomplish. A project scope statement is created at an early stage in the project to reflect the stakeholders' common understanding of major activities to be performed in the project, and to provide a basis for future project decisions. For internal projects, the scope is defined by the sponsor. For external projects, the scope is negotiated and agreed to by the external customer and internal sponsor. Scope does not include estimations of the cost of the work to be done or the time it will take to complete; those determinations are made separately.

Scope Definitions

Scope definitions are shaped by the deliverables, assumptions, and constraints that are documented during project initiation. At an organizational level, scope inputs include the organizational process assets (resources), the project charter (requirements, scope, and delivery factors), the preliminary project scope statement (project execution plan, phases, and delivery), the project scope management plan (evaluation, planning, execution, and launch), and the approved change requests (testing and quality assurance).

Target Audience

The target audience are individuals, groups, professionals, and communities to whom the project is delivered. Before creating a project plan, you need to identify the audience based on your project. After identifying the audience, you need to analyze them based on their age, gender, profession, culture, education, and various other factors. This analysis will help you understand your audience and their requirements so you can decide what information to present and how to present it.

Example for Ascertaining Design Elements

For example, if you are a graphic designer and if you were to build graphic illustrations for a course on Photoshop for students, then your design elements should be conceived, planned, designed, and developed in such a way that it is globally accepted and meets the student's learning objectives.

Project Management

Project management is the process of planning, organizing, and managing resources to ensure the successful completion of project goals and objectives. It also involves planning for infrastructure, risks, timelines, and other associated aspects that are integral to a project. Establishing regular monitoring mechanisms and test run of modules also forms an integral part of the project management process. Project management processes are grouped into different categories called process groups. The common process groups are initiating, planning, executing, monitoring, and closing. The process groups provide guidance in deploying the relevant project management skill and expertise during the project.

Common Problems and Issues

Organizations spend a huge amount of money on project initiatives. The return on such investments, however, is very minimal. Either the performance is poor or results are disappointing. Some of the common problems that organizations face in project management are:

* Unclear goals and objectives.
* Poor communication of objectives and targets across the team.
* Unclear responsibilities across the project.
* Lack of commitment or teamwork.

- Poor planning (quality, resource, and the like).

- Unofficial *scope creep* refers to the change in a project's scope after the project work has started. An example could be addition of new features to an already approved feature list. This could delay timelines and expand budgets.

Recommended Project Methods

Some of the recommended approaches or methods to creating an effective project plan include:

- Break down the planning task. Define the project (define goals, objectives, and benefits, and confirm delivery strategy) and then plan it (stage-wise delivery of the project).

- Check and validate the project delivery plan. Ensure that factors like resource planning, infrastructure required, budget, timelines, risk factors, contingencies, and all related delivery factors are chalked out before its commencement.

- Clearly communicate the roles, action, and responsibilities of each and every team member.

- Regularly monitor the progress in development, testing, and implementation.

- Clearly set quality standards of measurement for quality review.

- Test run completed modules for accuracy and immediate implementation.

 A technique called fast tracking in project management is used to compress project duration to shorten the project schedule so as to meet the target dates. This is usually done by compressing some of the project phases.

Approaches to Avoid

Some of the approaches that must be avoided in project management are:

- Do not overschedule your team members' time.

- Do not plan high and deliver small.

- Do not avoid risk management plans.

- Do not assume your audience, purpose, and goals.

ACTIVITY 1-1
Understanding a Project Plan

Scenario:
You are asked to work on a project plan to design a brochure. Before you start on the project, you want to review some of the elements of a well-designed project plan.

1. **What are the factors that need to be considered while planning a project? (Choose three.)**

   a) Design elements

   b) Geographical location where the project will be implemented

   c) Target audience

   d) Final output

2. **True or False? Scope definitions are shaped by deliverables, assumptions, and constraints that are documented during project initiation.**

   ___ True

   ___ False

TOPIC B

Identify Copyright and Citation Requirements

You examined the elements of a well-designed project plan and deliverables, and are ready to design a project. Before doing so, you need to know how to protect online information and to respect the rights of other content authors. In this topic, you will identify copyright and citation requirements.

With the vast wealth of information available on the Internet, it is easy to forget that not all of it is accurate or free for the taking. Unlike opening to the first pages of a book and seeing the printed copyright text, the copyright information of online content is not easily evident. To further complicate matters, it has become an all too common practice to download whatever content we want—images, music, and video that may or may not be legal to copy. Keeping up-to-date on copyright and citation requirements not only protects your information, but also acts as a reminder to respect that of others.

Copyright Terminology

Copyright refers to the rights given to the author of an original work for a set period of time. It applies to any form of work, idea, or information that is substantial and distinctive in any medium. When producing content for the web, it is important to understand and use copyright terms correctly.

Term	*Description*
Copyright	Enacted by Congress to protect the writing of authors. A copyright gives the owner exclusive rights to reproduce, distribute, perform, display, or license his work.
Copyrightable	Copyright works include: literary works, such as books, manuscripts, and computer programs; pictorial works, such as graphic art, photographs, and technical drawings; musical works (including drama), such as composition and lyrics, screenplays, and motion pictures; and sound recordings, such as music, audio (spoken) works, and sound effects.
Duration	The length of time a work can have copyrights. By default, the length of time is the life of the author plus 50 or 70 years. There are variations based on factors such as whether the work has been published and if both an individual and a company originated the copyright.
Fair use doctrine	Traditionally applied to academic use. For example: making and distributing copies of copyrighted works for teaching purposes.
Infringement	Unauthorized use of copyrighted material that violates any or all of the copyright owner's rights.

Term	Description
Intellectual property	Original thought/creative work (in tangible form) that is protected by law.
Derivative work	Work based upon a copyrighted work such as an update, revision, or adaptation.

Citations

Citations refer to an abbreviated expression that is included in any original intellectual work. It is usually included in the bibliographic references section of the work, especially where the relevance of the work of others specifically to the topic of discussion is acknowledged. The primary purpose of a citation is to attribute to other authors the ideas they have previously expressed.

Citation Systems

There are broadly two citation systems—Note systems and Parenthetical referencing. Note systems makes use of sequential numbers in the text, which are referred to as either footnotes or endnotes. An example of a footnote could be "1. Jane Holmes, On Graphic Tools—Level 1 (New Church: Sculls, 2009) 03–18." Parenthetical referencing is an alternative to using footnotes. It is used when you make reference to someone else's idea by quoting them directly using their name and page number of their work in the text of your work. An example of parenthetical referencing is "Photoshop is like painting a canvas on your computer. (Keith Steven 318)."

Copyright Permission

To use a copyrighted work, you need to obtain written permission from the copyright holder. It is recommended that your permission request includes the purpose, duration, and a description of how the material will be used. If you plan to use images or pictures from the web, you need to obtain a copyright or buy it. If a copyright holder cannot be located, you will not be able to use their images.

Locating Copyright Holders

Some of the sources you might use to locate the copyright holder from whom you want to secure permission include:

● Publisher of the work

● Webmaster of a website

● Photographer

● University or academic institution

● Researcher

● Designer

● Corporation/Company

The Copyright Notice

A statement indicating copyright ownership that includes the owner's name and the year the copyright was acquired is sometimes ample proof of copyright protection. However, the most visual and dependable way to show copyright ownership is the copyright notice. Often attached to a copyright work, the copyright notice includes:

- The word "Copyright"
- The copyright symbol ©
- The copyholder's name
- The statement "All rights reserved"

ACTIVITY 1-2
Reviewing Copyright and Citation Principles

Scenario:

As you become proficient in Photoshop, you will no doubt work with many multimedia assets for web production. During this creative process, it can be easy to forget about the legalities imposed on original and copied material. To ensure that you have a solid understanding of copyright and citation principles, you want to test your knowledge on them.

---

1. **You want to add a copyright statement to a website before publishing it. What statement elements are appropriate?**

    a) The copyright symbol (©)

    b) The state of origin

    c) The copyholder's name

    d) The word "Copyright"

    e) The statement "All rights reserved"

---

2. **While browsing images on the web, you come across an image that would be perfect for a web page you are working on. What action will you take to use the image?**

    a) Enlarge the image and copy it to your local system.

    b) Copy the image and make very slight changes so it is not like the original image.

    c) Check for copyright information and then contact the designer for permission.

    d) Check for copyright information, and if it is not evident, copy and use the image.

Lesson 1 Follow-up

In this lesson, you initiated a project by understanding its various factors, defining the scope of the project, and identifying copyright and citation information to use in a project. You will now be able to prepare a project plan and differentiate between original copyrighted material and plagiarized material.

1. **Why do you think planning is essential for any project?**

2. **Why do you think copyrighting a work and obtaining permission to use a copyrighted work are important?**

2 | Exploring the Adobe® Photoshop® CS5 Environment

Lesson Time: 1 hour(s), 20 minutes

Lesson Objectives:

In this lesson, you will explore the Adobe Photoshop CS5 environment.

You will:

● Explore the Photoshop interface.

● Customize the workspace.

● Explore Adobe Bridge.

Introduction

Before beginning to work with Adobe® Photoshop® CS5, you need to explore the interface elements to effectively use its built-in options and tools. Additionally, you may have to customize the appearance of the interface to your needs. In this lesson, you will explore and customize the Photoshop environment.

When learning to read, you first need to know the alphabet before you can string letters together to create a word or form a sentence. Learning to work with a new application such as Photoshop requires a similar approach. You need to know the basics before you can utilize the program to its full capabilities.

This lesson covers all or part of the following Adobe Visual Communication using Photoshop CS5 objectives:

● Topic A

■ Objective 3.1a: Identify and label elements of the Photoshop interface.

■ Objective 3.1b: Demonstrate knowledge of how to organize and customize the workspace.

■ Objective 3.1c: Demonstrate knowledge of the functions of tools on the Tools panel.

■ Objective 3.1d: Demonstrate knowledge of the functions of various panels.

■ Objective 3.1f: Demonstrate knowledge of navigating images, rotating the canvas, and using pan and zoom.

- Objective 4.1j: Demonstrate knowledge of how to use the Flash-based panels for manipulating SWF files.
- Objective 4.2d: Demonstrate knowledge of how to change the measurement unit on rulers.
- Objective 4.6c: Identify tools that are used for painting.
- Objective 4.6d: Identify tools that are used for drawing, or creating shapes.
- Topic B
  - Objective 3.1b: Demonstrate knowledge of how to organize and customize the workspace.

This lesson covers all or part of the following Adobe Photoshop CS5 ACE Exam objectives:

- Topic A
  - Objective 9.1 Use Mini-Bridge to view, manage, and open images inside Photoshop.
  - Objective 9.3 Work with tabbed documents and controls in the Application bar (options include tabbed documents, arrange documents menu, screen modes, canvas rotation, Application Frame, and n-up).
  - Objective 9.4 Given a scenario, choose an appropriate method to zoom and pan in the document window (options include the new scrubby zoom feature).
- Topic B
  - Objective 9.2 Describe how to arrange panels and manage workspaces (options include arranging and docking panels, customizing shortcuts, saving custom workspaces, using the workspace switcher).

TOPIC A
Explore the Photoshop Interface

You are preparing to explore how to create and edit images with Photoshop CS5. Before you can do that, you need to recognize the Photoshop environment and some of the tools you will use. In this topic, you will explore the Photoshop CS5 interface.

Managing your work area is an important aspect of working with Photoshop. Before you can do so, however, you need to become familiar with the Photoshop interface and its elements. Gaining this knowledge is the first step toward working with the application.

Adobe Photoshop CS5

Adobe Photoshop CS5 is an image-editing software application used by photographers, graphic designers, and web designers for image editing tasks such as creating composite images, making color correction, and enriching images with other visual effects. Photoshop contains a user-friendly environment with a set of well-defined tools and panels that are easily accessible and customizable. It supports a large number of image formats and high-end graphics for different media.

The Photoshop Window

The Photoshop CS5 window contains standard interface elements found in all Windows-based applications, but with additional tools and panels for creating, editing, and enhancing images.

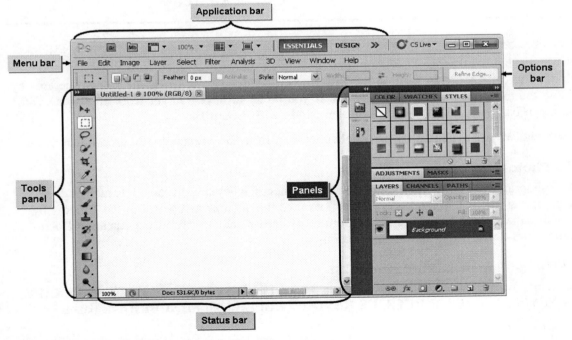

Figure 2-1: The Photoshop CS5 interface elements.

Interface Element	Description
Application bar	Consists of the menu bar and shortcuts to frequently used options. It also contains buttons to switch between workspaces, launch Adobe Bridge, access CS Live and the **MINI BRIDGE** panel, and change the document views, zoom level, and screen mode of a document.
Menu bar	Consists of menus.
Tools panel	Displays available tools in different sections.
Options bar	Appears below the Application bar and displays additional options for the currently selected tool.
Document window	Displays one or more files in a tabbed window. These tabbed windows can be arranged using various options. You can view, create, edit, and enhance images using this window.
Status bar	Appears at the bottom of the screen and displays the current magnification of the image. It consists of the File Information box, which contains information on the document size and storage size of the current image.
Panels	Comprise a group of panels with a tab for each panel. Most of the panels contain a menu, which allows you to perform additional tasks. Some of the panels are **ADJUSTMENTS, MASKS, LAYERS,** and **SWATCHES.**

Workspace Views

The Photoshop workspace has more than one default view. In addition to the **Standard Screen Mode,** you can choose to work in the **Full Screen Mode.** This enlarges the workspace area by hiding the menu bar, toolbars, and panels. If you prefer to have a larger work area along with the menu bar, you can choose **Full Screen Mode with Menu Bar.**

These choices are available on the Application bar, from the **Screen Mode** drop-down menu.

The Photoshop Document Window

Photoshop allows you to open multiple files or images. They are displayed as tabbed documents in the Photoshop interface. You can arrange the documents opened in the window by choosing the desired command either from the **Window** menu or from the **Arrange Documents** drop-down menu on the Application bar.

Additional Panels in Photoshop CS5

There are five panel extensions available in Adobe Photoshop CS5—the **ACCESS CS LIVE, CS NEWS AND RESOURCES, CS REVIEW, KULER,** and **MINI BRIDGE** panels.

The KULER Panel

The **KULER** panel provides access to the resources available on the Adobe Kuler website. You can browse, create, and share color themes online with other users of the Kuler website. You can also search for color themes based on keywords or criteria such as **Highly Rated, Most Popular, Newest, Random, Saved,** and **Custom.** Themes can be further filtered based on their creation time. You can also select a theme and add it to the **SWATCHES** panel.

Flash-Based Panels in Photoshop CS5

Photoshop CS5 allows you to use SWF panels created using the Flash application. If you are a programmer and an expert user of Flash, you can create an SWF panel and use it in Photoshop CS5. For example, you can create panels to sharpen images or photographs, increase the tone and clarity of the image, and enhance images. To make the SWF panels work in Photoshop, follow these steps:

- Create a ZIP file using the SWF files and the associated JavaScript files.
- Navigate to the C:\Program Files\Adobe Photoshop CS5\Plug-Ins\Panels folder.
- Copy the ZIP file and extract the files into the Panels folder.
- Restart the Photoshop CS5 application. The SWF panels will be available on the **Extensions** menu command.

Adobe CS Live Services

The Adobe CS Live services in Adobe Photoshop CS5 allow you to collaborate with peers and clients quickly and easily. It provides an online service that enables you to share designs or images instead of attaching huge files to email and logging on to FTP servers. With CS Live online services, you can get comments and feedback from the clients or reviewers immediately because review comments are displayed in near real time

CS REVIEW

CS Review is a quick and easy method to collaborate and stay connected using the services provided by the Adobe community. Adobe CS Review online service is designed to simplify and accelerate the design review process. The **CS REVIEW** panel allows you to share your projects and get feedback from peers and clients using a web browser.

The Tools Panel

The **Tools** panel displays all the available Photoshop tools organized into different sections.

Section	Description
Selection, manipulation, and utility tools	The selection tools allow you to make selections in an image and move selected areas to another image or within the same image.
	The manipulation tools allow you to select and cut or slice specific parts of an image.
	The utility tools allow you to make notes and voice annotations and select background and foreground colors.

Section	Description
Painting and retouching tools	The painting tools allow you to paint with brushes and create gradient files.
	The retouching tools allow you to correct and repair imperfections in images, take samples of images and paint copies of them elsewhere, erase pixels, and sharpen or blur images.
Drawing and type tools	The drawing tools allow you to select, create, and edit vector path segments and create shapes. Type tools allow you to add text to an image.
Navigation and 3D tools	The navigation tools allow you to scroll through an image and increase or decrease image magnification.
	3D tools allow you to rotate, roll, pan, slide, or scale three dimensional objects.
Color control tools	The color control tools display the current foreground and background colors and enable you to switch between them.
Mode control tool	The mode control tool allows you to make selections before editing or painting and creating temporary selection marks.

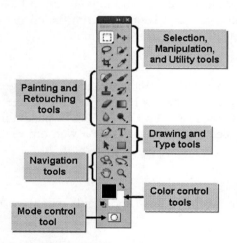

Figure 2-2: The Tools panel identified with its various sections.

Tool Groups

Some tool options include multiple, related tools that are grouped to form tool groups. These tools are indicated by a small arrow at the bottom-right corner of the tool. This arrow, when clicked, displays a flyout that contains a set of related tools. The **Tools** panel can be free floating or attached to the application window.

Navigation Tools

The navigation tools that are available in Photoshop are **Zoom** and **Hand.** Navigation tools are used to alter the position and zoom levels of the images in a document.

While the Zoom In tool is used to increase the magnification of the image, the Zoom Out tool is used to decrease the magnification. You can also select the **Zoom** tool and draw a marquee to enlarge a specific portion of the image. The **Hand** tool can be used to move and position an image within the window.

The NAVIGATOR Panel

The **NAVIGATOR** panel provides a number of options for quickly navigating through a document. The **View** box in this panel displays a miniature version of the image. This panel also has a **Zoom Slider** that can be used to quickly select a magnification level. However, you can use the **Zoom In** or **Zoom Out** button to change to the nearest preset zoom level. You can also specify a particular magnification value using the magnification text box located in the panel.

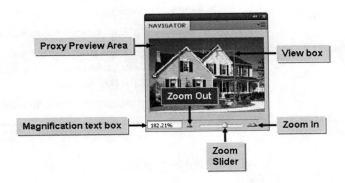

Figure 2-3: Options in the NAVIGATOR panel.

Zoom Percentage

The **Zoom** tool allows you to increase the magnification of an image up to 3200%.

Navigation Tools and Options

When you select either the **Pan** tool or the **Zoom** tool, the Options bar displays various options using which you can view the images in different sizes.

Option	Description
Actual Pixels	Displays images at 100%.
Fit Screen	Fits images to the screen.
Fill Screen	Fills images to the entire screen area.
Print Size	Displays images in the size of a printed output.

The MINI BRIDGE Panel

The **MINI BRIDGE** panel enables you to browse files from within the Photoshop application without having to launch the Bridge application. You can view the Bridge application in a miniature form inside this panel by choosing the commands from the **Panel View** drop-down menu. This panel also allows you to rename and preview the files, and publish images.

There are various other components available in the **MINI BRIDGE** panel. Some of them are described in the table.

Component	Used To
Back and forward buttons	Go backward and forward between the sections of the panel.
Go to parent, recent items, or Favorites drop-down list	Navigate to the files and folders that are recently opened, and to other locations such as source files, local drives, and other documents that are saved in the user machine.
Go to Adobe Bridge button	Launch the Adobe Bridge application.
Panel View drop-down menu	Display the **Path Bar, Navigation Pod,** and **Preview Pod** available in the Bridge application inside the **MINI BRIDGE** panel.
Search button	Search for the stored files using their titles.

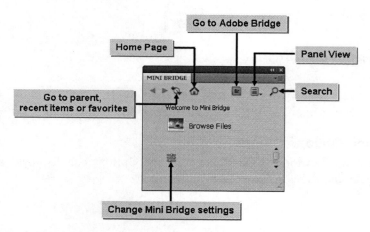

Figure 2-4: The MINI BRIDGE menu options.

How to Explore the Photoshop Interface

Procedure Reference: View Images Using the MINI BRIDGE Panel.

To view images using the **MINI BRIDGE** panel:

1. On the application bar, click the **Launch Mini Bridge** button.
2. Click **Browse Files.**
3. In the **CONTENT** section, navigate to the folder containing the images you wish to view.
4. If necessary, below the **MINI BRIDGE** panel, click the **View** button and from the pop-up menu, select the desired view mode.
   - Select **As List** to view images as a thumbnail along with their name and date of creation.
   - Select **As Details** to view images with details such as date of creation, date the image was modified, size and, file type.
   - Select **As Filmstrip** to view images along with their file name and extension as a filmstrip.
   - Select **As Thumbnails** to view images along with their file name and extension as a thumbnail.
   - Select **Grid Lock** to arrange images in a grid.
   - Select **Show Thumbnail Only** to view images as thumbnails without displaying their details.
   - Select **Show Items in Pages** to display images along with their file name and extension in pages.
5. If necessary, in the **CONTENT** section, from the **Select** drop-down menu, choose the desired command.
   - Choose **Refresh** to refresh the contents in the **CONTENT** section.
   - Choose **Show Reject Files** to display the files that are not in use or that have been labelled as rejected in Adobe Bridge.
   - Choose **Show Hidden Files** to display the hidden files.
   - Choose **Show Folders** to display the folders containing the images.
   - Choose **Select All** to select all the files in the **CONTENT** section.
   - Choose **Deselect All** to deselect all selected files in the **CONTENT** section.
   - Choose **Invert Selection** to return to the previous state of selection.

6. If necessary, in the **CONTENT** section, click the **Filter items by rating** drop-down arrow and choose the desired command.

    ● Choose **Clear Filter** to clear all filtering settings assigned to the files.

    ● Choose **Keep filter when browsing** to retain the filter settings assigned to the files.

    ● Choose **Show Rejected Items Only** to display only the files that are not in use or that have been labelled as rejected in Adobe Bridge.

    ● Choose **Show Unrated Items Only** to display only the files that have not been rated in Adobe Bridge.

    ● Choose the appropriate command to display files based on a single rating.

    ● Choose the appropriate command to display files based on multiple ratings.

    ● Choose **Show Labeled Items Only** to display only the labeled files.

    ● Choose **Show Unlabeled Items Only** to display only the unlabeled files.

7. If necessary, in the **CONTENT** section, from the **Sort** drop-down list, select the desired option for displaying the files.

8. If necessary, in the **CONTENT** section, from the **Tools** drop-down list, select the desired option.

    ● Select **Place** to display the files in the Photoshop application.

    ● Select **Photoshop** and select the desired option that would be used to process the files.

ACTIVITY 2-1
Exploring the Photoshop Interface

Data Files:

Paint Can.png

Scenario:

You are a new intern in the graphic design department of the company Kreativity@itsBest. On your first day, you learn that you will be required to use Photoshop CS5 to create a Color Sample Card for the Ristell Paints company. Because you are not familiar with this software, you decide to take a look at an image which your colleague has created to explore its features and options, and perhaps find some similarities to other applications you have worked with. Also, you want to look at the details of the design using various navigation tools in Photoshop, and then decide whether it needs to be modified to meet the client's requirements.

---

1. Open the Paint Can.png file in the Photoshop application to view it in different modes.

    a. Choose **Start→All Programs→Adobe Photoshop CS5** to launch the application.

    b. On the Application bar, on the menu bar, choose **File→Open.**

    c. In the **Open** dialog box, navigate to the C:\084384Data\Exploring the Adobe Photoshop Environment folder, select **Paint Can.png,** and click **Open.**

---

2. Compare the window display modes.

    a. On the Application bar, click **Screen Mode,**  and choose **Full Screen Mode With Menu Bar** to view the image at the center of the screen.

    b. On the Application bar, click **Screen Mode** and from the menu, choose **Full Screen Mode** to hide the window controls and the menu bar.

    c. In the **Message** message box, click **Full Screen** to view the image without panels and then press **Tab** to view the panels.

    d. From the **Screen Mode** drop-down menu, choose **Standard Screen Mode** to view the image with the window controls and the menu bar.

---

3. Magnify the image using the **Zoom** tool to view the image clearly.

    a. In the **Tools** panel, select the **Zoom** tool.

    b. Observe that the mouse pointer in the document window has changed to a magnifying glass.

    c.   On the image, click the text **"HEXA"** to change the zoom percentage to 200%.

    d.   Hold down the **Alt** key. Observe that the Plus Sign **(+)** in the magnifying glass has changed to a Minus Sign **(-).** Click the image two times.

    e.   At the bottom-left corner of the window, in the magnification text box, verify that the zoom percentage is displayed as **66.67%.**

4.   Zoom in on the image using the **NAVIGATOR** panel for a better view.

    a.   Choose **Window→Navigator** to display the **NAVIGATOR** panel in the right side of the window.

    b.   In the **NAVIGATOR** panel, to the right of the slider, click the **Zoom In** button, twice to increase the zoom percentage to 200%.

    c.   In the **NAVIGATOR** panel, in the magnification text box, double-click, type *300* and then press **Enter.**

5.   Scroll through the image using the **NAVIGATOR** panel to view the particular portion of an image.

    a.   In the **NAVIGATOR** panel, in the **Proxy Preview Area,** position the mouse pointer in the red outlined portion and observe that the mouse pointer changes to a hand cursor.

    b.   Drag the red outline over the text at the bottom of the can to get a closer view of it.

    c.   In the **NAVIGATOR** panel, in the magnification text box, double-click, type *100* and then press **Enter.**

TOPIC B
Customize the Workspace

You explored the Photoshop interface. However, when specific elements needed for a particular task are organized on screen, you can easily navigate through the application. In this topic, you will customize the workspace.

Imagine having a workspace cluttered with different tools and panels. You will have a difficult time navigating and locating the tools you want. Customizing the Photoshop interface allows you to easily access the required tools.

Predefined Workspaces

Predefined workspaces are presets that contain customized interface elements. In Photoshop, there are a collection of *workspace presets* available, which are created specific to tasks such as 3D, designing, videos, painting, or photography. You can apply any workspace preset to the application to suit your needs, using the **Window** menu or the workspace switcher on the Application bar.

Custom Workspaces

You can rearrange a workspace to best suit your creative workflow by moving, hiding, or displaying panels. The panels can be docked, undocked, collapsed, or presented as icons or as icons with labels. You can create a customized workspace and activate it any time. You can also switch from one workspace to another, modify a workspace, and reset or delete a customized workspace. The live workspace feature in Photoshop CS5 automatically saves the changes that are made to a particular workspace. This allows you to switch to other workspaces and return to a workspace to find the same panel arrangement you had earlier been working with.

Workspace Switcher

In Photoshop CS5, you can customize the workspace switcher on the Application bar. You can change the number of workspaces displayed, select the workspaces you want to be displayed, and also change the order of workspaces displayed in the workspace switcher drop-down list.

The Keyboard Shortcuts and Menus Dialog Box

You can customize the keyboard shortcuts and menus in Adobe Photoshop by using the **Keyboard Shortcuts and Menus** dialog box. The **Keyboard Shortcuts** tab contains options that allow you to define new shortcuts or delete existing ones for the application menus, panel menus, and tools. The **Menus** tab enables you to customize menus, choose color coding for menu commands, and change their visibility.

Custom Panels with Configurator 2.0

Photoshop CS5 allows you to use customized panels to extend the functionality of a workspace. You can create your own panels with Configurator 2.0, a panel utility, that can be downloaded from the Adobe website. Using this utility, you can combine various tools, options, and commands into a single panel. You can also display content from the web such as web feeds, blogs, videos, and email in these panels. Panels that are created can be shared with other Photoshop users too.

The Preferences Dialog Box

The **Preferences** dialog box allows you to set various options for the general display and appearance of the interface.

Option	Allows You To
General	Specify settings for the color picker and zoom. You can also reset the settings for warning messages so that it will not be displayed while working.
Interface	Specify settings for the display of the screen, panels, and documents. It also allows you to select the font size and the required language.
File Handling	Specify settings for saving files and file compatibility.
Performance	Specify settings for memory usage, history and cache, scratch disks, and GPU settings.
Cursors	Specify settings for painting cursors and other cursors.
Transparency and Gamut	Specify settings for transparency background and gamut warning.
Units & Rulers	Specify settings for the display of units, column size, new document preset resolutions, and point/pica size.
Guides, Grid & Slices	Specify settings for color and style of guides, smart guides, grids, and slices.
Plug-Ins	Specify settings for panel extensions and additional plug-ins.
Type	Specify settings for type characters such as smart quotes, Asian text, font names in English, and more.
3D	Specify settings such as VRAM space for 3D, interactive rendering, 3D overlays, 3D file loading, and more.

File Saving

In Photoshop CS5, there are two options for saving a file. The default option takes you to the original folder from where the file has been opened. However, you can change the file saving preference by unchecking the **Save as to Original Folder** check box to save the file in a different location.

The Preset Manager

The **Preset Manager** enables you to choose your own workspace customization from a library of preset panels. The **Preset Manager** provides you with options that can be used to replace the existing panel contents by loading another preset panel file. You can also restore the panel to its default state.

The Preset Manager Menu

The **Preset Manager** dialog box contains a menu that allows you to change the way items in the panels are displayed. You can:

- Decide the way the preset type will be displayed on the Options bar, panels, or dialog boxes.
- Reset the panel to its default or replace a panel with another panel from the folder.
- Choose from libraries of preset brushes, gradients, styles, swatches, patterns, custom shapes, contours, and tools. You can either change the default preset items or create libraries.

How to Customize the Workspace

Procedure Reference: Customize the Panel Arrangement

To customize the panel arrangement:

1. Launch the Adobe Photoshop CS5 application.
2. Customize the panel arrangement.
   - From the **Window** menu, choose a panel to display it.
   - Arrange the panels as desired.
     - Select a panel tab and drag it next to the tabs within a group to group the panels.
     - In a panel group, click a panel tab and drag it away from the group to ungroup a panel from it.
     - Select a panel tab, drag it to the top or bottom of the panel group until a horizontal line appears, and release the mouse button to dock the panel with another panel or group.
     - Click and drag a panel tab away from the panel to which it is docked, to undock the panel.
     - Double-click a panel tab to collapse or expand the panel.
     - On the gray area of the panel, click the double arrow to display the panel or panel group as icons.

        You can drag the corner of the panel group to display the panel group as icons with labels.

   - Close a panel.
     - From the panel options menu, choose **Close** to close the selected panel or;
     - Right-click the panel tab and from the displayed menu, choose **Close.**
   - Close a panel group.

- From the panel options menu, choose **Close Tab Group** to close a group of panels or;
- Right-click the panel tab and from the displayed menu, choose **Close Tab Group.**

Procedure Reference: Customize Workspace Keyboard Shortcuts and Menus

To customize the workspace keyboard shortcuts and menus:

1. Choose **Window→Workspace→Keyboard Shortcuts & Menus** to display the **Keyboard Shortcuts and Menus** dialog box.
2. On the **Menus** tab, from the **Set** drop-down list, select the workspace that you want to modify.
3. From the **Menu For** drop-down list, select the desired option.
   - Select **Application Menus** to customize an application menu.
   - Select **Panel Menus** to customize a panel menu.
4. In the **Menu Command** row, expand a menu to view its commands.
5. If necessary, make the necessary changes to a menu command.
   - Hide a command.
      a. Select a menu command.
      b. In the **Visibility** section, click the eye icon of the menu command to hide it.
   - Add color to a menu command.
      a. Select a menu command.
      b. In the **Color** section, click **None,** and from the drop-down list, select the desired color to add it to the menu command.
6. Click the **Create a new set based on the current set of menus** button.
7. In the **Save** dialog box, in the **File name** text box, type the desired name for the custom set and click **Save.**

 If you want to modify an existing Photoshop Default set, do not name the new set. Instead, click the **Save all changes to the current set of menus** button and then click **OK.**

8. If necessary, delete a saved set.
   a. On the **Menus** tab, from the **Set** drop-down list, select the set you want to delete.
   b. Click the **Delete the current set of menus** button.
   c. In the **Keyboard Shortcuts and Menus** message box, click **Yes.**
9. In the **Keyboard Shortcuts and Menus** dialog box, click **OK.**

The Menu Commands

The **Menu** commands include both the application and panel menus. An example of an application menu command is the **File** menu. When you expand the **File** menu, you can make changes to commands such as **New, Open, Close,** and **Close All.**

Procedure Reference: Customize the Workspace Switcher

To customize the workspace switcher:

1. If necessary, on the Application bar, click the **Drag to resize** partition line to expand the workspace switcher.

2. In the workspace switcher section, click the **Show more workspaces and options** arrow and from the drop-down list, select the desired workspace preset.

 The selected workspace preset will be displayed in the workspace switcher section of the Application bar.

3. If necessary, in the workspace switcher section, click and drag the workspace and place it in the desired location to rearrange the order of workspaces displayed.

Procedure Reference: Save a Workspace

To save a workspace:

1. Choose a workspace preset.
    *   Choose **Window→Workspace** and choose the desired workspace preset or;
    *   On the Application bar, from the workspace switcher drop-down list, select the desired preset.

2. Make necessary changes to the panel arrangement, keyboard shortcuts, and menus.

3. Choose **Window→Workspace→New Workspace.**

4. In the **New Workspace** dialog box, in the **Name** text box, type the desired name for the new workspace.

5. In the **Capture** section, check the desired check box to save the panel locations, keyboard shortcuts, and menus.

6. Click **Save.**

7. If necessary, delete a workspace.
    a. Choose **Window→Workspace→Delete Workspace.**
    b. In the **Delete Workspace** dialog box, from the **Workspace** drop-down list, select the workspace you want to delete and click **Delete.**
    c. In the **Delete Workspace** message box, click **Yes.**

Procedure Reference: Load Preset Options Using the Preset Manager

To load preset options using the **Preset Manager:**

1. Choose **Edit→Preset Manager.**

2. In the **Preset Manager** dialog box, from the **Preset Type** drop-down list, select the desired preset type.

3. Click **Load.**

4. In the **Load** dialog box, select a library file you want to load and then click **Load.**

5. In the **Preset Manager** dialog box, click **Done.**

6. If necessary, select any item in the panel and click the **Rename** button to rename it.

7. If necessary, select any item in the panel and click the **Delete** button to delete it.

Procedure Reference: Reset the Preset Options to Photoshop Defaults

To reset the preset options to Photoshop defaults:

1. Choose **Edit→Preset Manager.**

2. From the **Preset Type** drop-down list, select the preset that needs to be reset with default options.

3. Click the triangle at the right of the **Preset Type** drop-down list.

4. From the drop-down list, select **Reset <Preset Type>.**

5. In the **Preset Manager** message box, click **OK.**

6. In the **Preset Manager** dialog box, click **Done.**

ACTIVITY 2-2
Customizing the Photoshop Environment

Data Files:

Paint Can.png

Before You Begin:

The Paint Can.png file is open.

Scenario:

You need to create a color sample card for Ristell Paints using the Photoshop application. The Photoshop environment you are working with is cluttered with components that you will not need for this project, so you decide to arrange the workspace components to suit your needs. You want to have easy access to tools that you will use frequently. Because you anticipate working on similar projects, you know that saving your custom workspace will save you time in the future.

1. Customize the position and appearance of the Photoshop interface elements to save it as a custom workspace.

    a. At the top-left corner of the **Tools** panel, in the gray area, click the right-pointing arrows, [▸▸] to display the **Tools** panel in two columns.

    b. At the top-right corner of the **ADJUSTMENTS** panel group, click the button with a small arrow, [▾≡] and choose **Close Tab Group** to close the panel group.

    c. Click and drag the **STYLES** panel and place it below the **LAYERS** panel group as a separate panel.

    d. Right-click the **COLOR** panel tab and choose **Close Tab Group** to close the panel group.

    e. Select the **PATHS** panel and at the right corner of the tab, from the panel options menu, choose **Close** to close the panel.

f.   Drag the **NAVIGATOR** panel and place it to the right of the **CHANNELS** panel.

g.   Close the **HISTOGRAM** panel group.

h.   Click the **Expand Panels** button of the docked panel group to display the **MINI BRIDGE** panel and the **HISTORY** panel.

i.   Close the **MINI BRIDGE** panel and the **HISTORY** panel.

2.   Set ruler options for the workspace to suit your project.

a.   Choose **Edit→Preferences→Units & Rulers.**

b.   In the **Preferences** dialog box, in the **Units** section, from the **Rulers** drop-down list, select **pixels.**

c.   From the **Type** drop-down list, verify that **points** is displayed.

d.   Click **OK.**

3.   Add color emphasis to the **Open** command and hide the **Check In** command on the **File** menu.

a.   On the menu bar, click **File** to display its commands.

b.   Observe the **Open** and **Check In** commands.

c.   Choose **Window→Workspace→Keyboard Shortcuts & Menus.**

d.   In the **Keyboard Shortcuts and Menus** dialog box, verify that the settings for **Photoshop Defaults** and **Application Menus** are displayed.

e.   In the **Application Menu Command** column, expand **File.**

f.   In the **Color** column of the **Open** command, click **None,** and from the drop-down list, select **Red.**

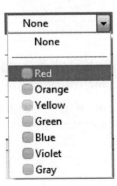

g.   Scroll down to display the **Check In** command and click the eye icon to hide the menu command.

4.   Create a set of menus and save the changes.

a.   To the right of the **Set** drop-down list, click the **Create a new set based on the current set of menus** button.

b.   In the **Save** dialog box, in the **File name** text box, type *My File Menu* and click **Save.**

c.   In the **Keyboard Shortcuts and Menus** dialog box, click **OK** to save the changes.

d.   Click **File.**

e.   Verify that the **Open** command is highlighted in red and the **Check In** command is not appearing.

f.   Click anywhere in the application to collapse the **File** menu.

5.   Save the customized workspace.

a.   Choose **Window→Workspace→New Workspace.**

b.   In the **New Workspace** dialog box, in the **Name** text box, type *My Workspace*

c.   In the **Capture** section, check the **Menus** check box.

d.   Click **Save.**

e.   Choose **File→Close** to close the file.

TOPIC C
Explore Adobe Bridge

You customized the Photoshop CS5 interface. Now, you want to become familiar with file management utility in Photoshop. In this topic, you will explore Adobe Bridge.

Although Photoshop allows you to work with files of different formats, it can be tedious to organize files, especially if they are numerous. Adobe Bridge offers a central location for keeping your files organized and provides options for asset management.

Adobe Bridge

Adobe Bridge is a file browser that allows you to view, sort, and manage both Adobe and non-Adobe application files from within a central location. It also allows you to create and manage folders, and rename, move, or delete files. You can also add and edit keywords and metadata; preview, rotate, and rank assets; and run batch commands. Adobe Bridge includes a search feature that allows multiple search criteria parameters.

Adobe Version Cue and Adobe Stock Photos

Adobe Bridge allows direct access to both Adobe® Version Cue®, Photoshop's project management feature, and Adobe® Stock Photos, a service that allows you to search, test, and purchase stock images.

Adobe Bridge Components

The Adobe Bridge interface elements allow you to display and organize files.

Interface Component	Description
Menu bar	Contains menu commands that enable you to view and edit elements in Adobe Bridge.
Panels groups	Contain panels with a separate tab for each panel. Panels include **FOLDERS, FAVORITES, METADATA, KEYWORDS, FILTER, PREVIEW, INSPECTOR,** and **COLLECTIONS.**
Tool bar	Comprises the navigation buttons, workspace presets, screen mode options, and a search text box.
Path Bar	Contains options to create and delete folders and sort files as well.
View bar	Contains buttons for displaying folders.

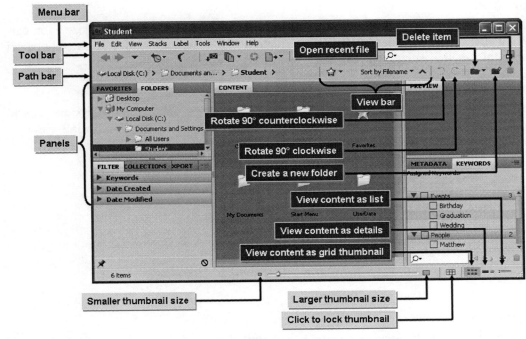

Figure 2-5: The Adobe Bridge application displaying its interface elements.

Views in Adobe Bridge

Adobe Bridge offers several options for viewing files and folders.

View Option	Description
Slideshow	Enables you to view a slide show of all the files.
Review Mode	Displays window content as a collection that is displayed like a stack of cards.
Compact Mode	Reduces the Bridge to a small window size that can be floated like a panel.
As Thumbnails	Displays only a thumbnail of each file.
As Details	Displays the date and time of creation and modification of the files.
As List	Displays the files as a list.
Show Hidden Files	Displays hidden files such as cache files and provisionally removed Version Cue files.
Show Folders	Displays folders and files.
Show Items from Subfolders	Displays contents from within folders.
Sort	Selects the order in which files are displayed. Files can be sorted in ascending or descending order, or manually.

The Sort Options

Files can be sorted by specifying file information such as the file name and file size. You can also sort by specifying the dates of document creation and document modification or by specifying other information such as dimensions, resolution, and color profile.

The View As Options

Adobe Bridge offers several options for viewing the workspace. The default views are **Thumbnail** and **Details**. The **Details** view displays items in a grid, whereas the **Thumbnail** view displays a list of thumbnails with information about each file.

How to Explore Adobe Bridge

Procedure Reference: Explore Adobe Bridge

To explore Adobe Bridge:

1. Launch Adobe Bridge.

   - On the Application bar, click the **Launch Bridge** button or;
   - Choose **File→Browse in Bridge.**

2. Explore Adobe Bridge.

   - Navigate to folders using the panels and **Path bar.**
     - On the **Path bar,** click the folder names to navigate to the desired folder or;
     - In the **FAVORITES** panel, navigate to the desired folder or;
     - In the **FOLDER** panel, navigate to the desired folder.
   - On the **Path Bar,** click the desired button.
     - Click the **Create a new folder** button to create a folder.
     - Click the **Open recent file** button and from the drop-down list, select the desired file.
     - Click the **Delete item** button to delete the selected file.
   - Choose **Window→Workspace** to display a list of workspaces.
   - From the **View** menu, choose the view that you want the files to be displayed in.

ACTIVITY 2-3
Exploring Adobe Bridge

Scenario:
The support files or assets of the color sample card are placed in different folders on your local system. Now, you want to manage the assets you will use for creating the color sample card using Adobe Bridge. Before you begin with this task, you want to explore Adobe Bridge.

---

1. Display Adobe Bridge and locate the Paint Can.png file.

   a. Choose **File→Browse in Bridge.**

   b. In the **Adobe Bridge** message box, click **No.**

   c. In the left side of the interface, select the **FOLDERS** panel to activate the panel.

   d. In the **FOLDERS** panel, select **My Computer** to display its content in the **CONTENT** panel.

   e. In the **CONTENT** panel, double-click the **Local Disk (C:)** drive to display its contents.

   f. In the **CONTENT** panel, double-click the **084384Data** folder to view its contents.

---

2. View the details of the files in the **CONTENT** panel.

   a. On the menu bar, choose **View→As Details** to display additional information about the folders.

   b. Scroll-down, double-click the **Exploring the Adobe Photoshop Environment** folder.

   c. Double-click the **Support Files** folder.

   d. Choose **View→As List** to list the items in the **CONTENT** panel.

   e. Select the **Magenta Paint Can.png** file to preview it in the **PREVIEW** panel.

   f. Choose **File→Exit** to close Adobe Bridge.

Lesson 2 Follow-up

In this lesson, you explored the Adobe Photoshop CS5 environment, customized the Photoshop workspace, and worked with the navigation tools. Familiarizing yourself with the Photoshop environment and the basic tools and features, makes it easier for you to get started with creating and developing a project using Photoshop.

1. Which of the Photoshop application tools will you use often? Why?

2. How does customizing the Photoshop environment benefit you?

3 | Determining Graphic Type and Resolution

Lesson Time: 20 minutes

Lesson Objectives:

In this lesson, you will determine the resolution and graphic type.

You will:

- Identify the difference between raster and vector graphics.
- Understand image resolution.

Introduction

You explored the various components of the Photoshop environment and customized the workspace. The essence of Photoshop lies in its vibrant graphics that when explored offer a collage of pictures giving an experience similar to working on a piece of art. In this lesson, you will be enlightened on the basics of image resolution and graphic types that include learning to determine the appropriate image resolution and graphic type.

You may need to adjust image size and resolution, or select a specific type of graphic designed for image sharpness and clarity. Photoshop offers a number of tools and features that allow you to work with image resolution and graphic type.

This lesson covers all or part of the following Adobe Visual Communication using Photoshop CS5 objectives:

- Topic B
    - Objective 2.1a: Demonstrate knowledge of how image resolution can change once an image is manipulated.
    - Objective 2.1c: Identify appropriate image formats for web, video, photos, print, PowerPoint, or Word.
    - Objective 2.1d: Identify the difference between image size measured in pixels and document size measured in inches.
    - Objective 2.5e: Identify the most appropriate image type to use in a variety of situations.
    - Objective 4.3g: Demonstrate knowledge of how to resample to a larger or smaller image.

■ Objective 4.3h: Demonstrate knowledge of how to crop and how to resample an image.

This lesson covers all or part of the following Adobe Photoshop CS5 ACE Exam objectives:

● Topic A

■ Objective 4.2 Describe the difference between pixel-based and vector-based images.

■ Objective 9.9 Understand common file formats and the pros and cons of saving an image in those formats.

● Topic B

■ Objective 9.6 Given a scenario, properly resize an image (options include Image Size dialog box, resampling controls, Canvas Size dialog box, Transform options, Crop tool, and Content Aware Scale).

TOPIC A

Differentiate Between Raster and Vector Graphics

You explored the various components of the Photoshop interface. But before you begin working on a project, you need to plan for resources and deliverables that may include identifying and using the right graphic type. In this topic, you will differentiate between raster and vector graphics.

Photoshop is a popular and widely used application that enables professionals, students, and many others to create graphical outputs in varied forms and types. These may include retouched and color corrected photographs, photo illustrations, realistic simulations of traditional painting and drawing media, and computer effects. Before you work with graphic images, it is important to determine whether images are made up of pixels (raster) or geometric shapes (vector).

Pixels

Definition:

Pixels, short for picture elements, are square dots that you see on an image when you zoom in to high magnification. Each pixel within an image can be of a different color or shade of gray. The number of bits used to represent each pixel determines how many colors or shades of gray can be displayed.

The resolution of a Photoshop image is measured in *pixels per inch (ppi)*. It is calculated by dividing the pixels spread horizontally and vertically in a digital photo by the actual length or width of a printed image.

Example:

Pixalated portion of the house with zoom increased several times   Original image

Figure 3-1: *The image on the left shows a pixelated portion of the house with the zoom increased several times.*

Raster Graphics

Definition:

Raster graphics are images that are composed of a grid or raster of small squares called *pixels*. When you enlarge a raster graphic, you can see each pixel, which gives the graphic a jagged appearance. Raster graphics are more suitable for retouching, photo processing, and photorealistic illustrations. Raster graphics can be saved in file formats such as *Bitmap (BMP)*, *Tagged Image File Format (TIFF)*, and *Joint Photographic Experts Group (JPG)*. Most images that are viewed on the computer or on the web are raster graphics. Because they contain many pixels, their memory and storage space would increase or decrease based on the image size. To maintain a consistent file size format, several image compression algorithms have been developed. The most popular and common compressed image formats are JPEG and GIF.

Example:

Resizing the graphic results in loss of quality

Figure 3-2: A raster graphic that affects image quality when resized.

Vector Graphics

Definition:

Vector graphics are lines, curves, or other geometric shapes that are defined by a set of mathematical instructions. They are not pixelated and can be easily moved or modified without losing their original details or clarity. They are best suited for graphic designs, page layouts, typography, logos, and sharp-edged artistic illustrations such as cartoons and clip art. Vector graphics can be saved in different file formats such as *Encapsulated PostScript (EPS)*, *Portable Document Format (PDF)*, and *Scalable Vector Graphics (SVG)*.

Example:

Resizing the graphic retains quality

Figure 3-3: A vector graphic that retains image quality when resized.

ACTIVITY 3-1
Differentiating Raster and Vector Graphics

Scenario:

A team member tells you that the image you are working with is a vector graphic. Because you are new to vector graphics, you decide to explore the different types of graphics that you might be working with in Photoshop. Hence, you decide to test your knowledge on the understanding of different graphic types.

1. **True or False? Vector graphics are composed of mathematically defined shapes.**

    ___ True

    ___ False

2. **True or False? Raster graphics require less memory and storage to manipulate them.**

    ___ True

    ___ False

3. **Which statements about raster graphics are true?**

    a) Raster graphics are composed of a grid of pixels.

    b) Raster graphics are composed of lines defined by a set of mathematical instructions.

    c) Raster graphics can be created using the Photoshop application.

    d) Raster graphics are composed of curves and geometrical shapes.

TOPIC B
Understand Image Resolution

You identified the differences between raster and vector graphics. Before working with images, however, you must understand that the quality of an image depends on its size and resolution. In this topic, you will understand image resolution.

Creating an image for commercial or professional purposes requires knowledge of more than just paper size and orientation. Similarly, creating an image for the web requires knowledge of file properties and website considerations. An important factor in creating visually appealing images for both print and web is knowing how to optimize image resolution and size.

Image Resolution

Image resolution is an image holding attribute that determines the sharpness and clarity of an image. It denotes the number of pixels in the horizontal or vertical direction within an image when it is printed. It is measured in ppi. The greater the ppi of an image, the higher the resolution, quality, and the larger the file size. You can obtain information on the image resolution from the **Image Size** dialog box.

Figure 3-4: A pixelated portion of an image.

Image Manipulation

In Photoshop, images can be manipulated using various tools and features to obtain the desired output. The manipulation of images, however, does not affect image resolution. Manipulating images will result in pixel values changing or even the addition and removal of pixels. Though this may cause the image to lose clarity, its resolution remains unchanged. Image resolution can only be changed using the **Image Size** dialog box and specifying the desired resolution.

Image Size

Image size is determined by pixel dimensions. *Pixel dimensions* are the number of pixels that make up the height and width of an image. You can view the size of an image in the file information box on the status bar, or by using the **Image Size** command on the **Image** menu.

The Image Size Dialog Box

The **Image Size** dialog box displays the pixel dimensions and the print size of an image. It can be used to resize an image with or without changing the pixel dimensions and file size. You can also modify the size and resolution of an image.

File Size

One of the main objectives when creating web graphics is to keep the file size as small as possible. The larger the file size, the longer it takes for the viewer to download the file. Some of the main factors that contribute to the file size are the number of pixels, colors used, image compression, and additional information stored in the file.

Measurements

Image sizes can be measured in pixels or inches. Measuring an image in pixels will provide information on the number of pixels arranged horizontally and vertically on the image. It does not, however, indicate the size of the image in a unit of measurement you are familiar with such as inches or centimeters. The dimension of the image can be calculated using the measurement in pixels and the resolution of the image. The width of the image will be the number of pixels along the horizontal axis divided by the resolution of the image. Similarly, the height can also be calculated. Dimensions when indicated in inches or centimeters or any other familiar unit of measurement express exactly the image dimensions.

The resolution of an image largely impacts the pixel dimensions and the document size. While image size measured in pixels and the resolution indicates the quality of the image, document size measured in inches determines the size of the image when it is output.

Photoshop File Formats

Photoshop can save images in several file formats. Some file formats such as TIFF, EPS, and PDF are most appropriate for printing or exporting to page layout applications, while others such as GIF and JPEG are typically used for adding images on web pages. However, in Photoshop, files will be saved in the native format (*.PSD or *.PDD), because it retains all the original information without affecting its quality.

Image File Formats used in Other Applications

Image file formats are not always compatible with a variety of applications. For example, Office productivity applications, such as PowerPoint and Word, support JPEG, TIFF, PNG, BMP, EPS, GIF, and PICT formats.

How to Understand Image Resolution

Procedure Reference: Determine the Image Size in Photoshop

To determine the image size in Photoshop:

1. On the status bar, in the file information area, click the triangle.
2. From the menu, choose **Document Dimensions** to view the size of the image on the status bar.

Resampling Images Using the Image Size Dialog Box

The resampling option in the **Image Size** dialog box allows you to change the pixel dimensions of an image. In the **Image Size** dialog box, the resampling option is turned on by default. You can resample images by changing the pixel dimension, size, or resolution. Changing any one value will affect the other values, especially pixel dimensions. The pixel dimensions and the file size will change, and Photoshop must recreate the same image appearance using a different set of pixels. Resampling affects both the onscreen display and the printed images. The process of resampling is based on whether the image is scaled smaller (downsampling) or larger (upsampling). In Photoshop CS5, there are five methods to resample an image.

Method	Description
Nearest Neighbor	Used to resize illustrations but it can make jagged edges.
Bilinear	Gives an average result by balancing the speed and quality based on the image pixels.
Bicubic	A slow-paced method but it can produce more precise effect. This method determines the values of pixels by calculating the average weight of the closest pixels to produce smoother results.
Bicubic Smoother	An improved Bicubic method, and it is especially designed to enlarge images (upsampling).
Bicubic Sharper	An improved Bicubic method that is designed to reduce the size of images (downsampling).

Procedure Reference: Change the Print Dimensions and Resolution of an Image

To change the print dimensions and resolution of an image:

1. Open the desired image.
2. Choose **Image→Image Size.**
3. In the **Image Size** dialog box, specify the desired settings.
   - In the **Pixel Dimensions** section of the **Image Size** dialog box, specify the pixel dimensions for the image.
     - In the **Width** text box, type the required value, and from its corresponding drop-down list, select the required unit of measurement.
     - In the **Height** text box, type the required value, and from its corresponding drop-down list, select the required unit of measurement.
   - Check the **Scale Styles** check box to preserve the appearance of the effects applied to the image.
   - Check the **Constrain Proportions** check box to maintain the width in proportion to the height of the image.

 This option will automatically update the width of the image as you change its height, and vice versa.

   - If necessary, specify the resampling settings.
     - Check the **Resample Image** check box to change the print dimensions and the resolution of the image, and adjust the total number of pixels in the image proportionately.
     - Uncheck the **Resample Image** check box to change the print dimensions and the resolution of the image without changing the total number of pixels in the image.

- In the **Document Size** section, in the **Width** and **Height** text boxes, type the width and height values, respectively.

- In the **Document Size** section, in the **Resolution** text box, type a value to set the resolution of the image and click **OK.**

4. Choose **View→Print Size** to ascertain the print size of the image after specifying the settings.

5. If necessary, view the image at 100 percent magnification and notice the change in its resolution.

6. If necessary, choose **Edit→Undo Image Size** to remove the image adjustments if you are not satisfied with the output.

ACTIVITY 3-2
Understanding Image Resolution

Data Files:

Home.jpg

Before You Begin:

Navigate to the C:\084384Data\Determining Resolution and Graphic Type folder and open the Home.jpg file.

Scenario:

To create the color sample card, you decide to begin by importing the main background image for the outer page. The image has high resolution, making it too large. You decide to change the resolution to meet the expected quality and file size to suit the cover page design.

---

1. Change the resolution of the image to meet image size requirements.

   a. Choose **Image→Image Size.**

   b. In the **Image Size** dialog box, in the **Pixel Dimensions: 22.1M** section, verify that in the **Width** and **Height** text boxes, the values **2267** and **3408** are displayed respectively.

   c. In the **Document Size** section, in the **Resolution** text box, double-click and type **508**

   d. In the **Pixel Dimensions** section, verify that the width and height values have been proportionately reduced, and click **OK.**

---

2. Save the file as **Home Resized.psd**

   a. Choose **File→Save As.**

   b. In the **Save As** dialog box, in the **File name** text box, type **Home Resized**

   c. From the **Format** drop-down list, select **Photoshop (*.PSD;*.PDD).**

   d. Click **Save.**

   e. On the Home Resized.psd tab, click the close button to close the file.

---

3. **True or False? A greater ppi results in higher resolution and quality but smaller file size.**

   ___ True

   ___ False

Lesson 3 Follow-up

In this lesson, you determined various features and functions of graphic types and image resolution in Photoshop. This allows you to identify and use an appropriate graphic type and modify the sharpness and clarity of an image selected.

1.   **Which graphic type do you expect to work with often? Why?**

2.   **How will your knowledge on image resolution help you when working with images?**

4 Working with Selections

Lesson Time: 1 hour(s), 25 minutes

Lesson Objectives:

In this lesson, you will work with selections.

You will:

- Use different tools in Photoshop to select parts of images.
- Save a selection.
- Modify a selection.
- Apply color to a selection.

Introduction

You determined the image resolution and graphic types to work with different images. Now, you may want to use the tools in Photoshop to create selections on images. In this lesson, you will work with selections.

Photoshop has a number of tools that serve specific purposes. For instance, instead of working on an entire image, you might want to work on a part of the image and make modifications to it. However, if the selection is not made accurately, the edited result could look sloppy, grainy, or unrealistic. Being able to employ the appropriate tools to select and make image modifications is an important skill to obtain.

This lesson covers all or part of the following Adobe Visual Communication using Photoshop CS5 objectives:

- Topic A
    - Objective 3.3a: Demonstrate knowledge of how to import, export, and save files.
    - Objective 4.1a: Demonstrate knowledge of making selections using a variety of tools.
    - Objective 4.1c: Demonstrate knowledge of moving, copying, and pasting selections.
    - Objective 4.1d: Demonstrate knowledge of selection commands and how to modify selections.
    - Objective 4.1e: Identify when to use feathering and anti-aliasing when making selections.
    - Objective 4.1f: Identify tools that are used for selection.

- Objective 4.2a: Demonstrate knowledge of how to show and hide rulers.
- Objective 4.2b: Demonstrate knowledge of how to add and remove guides.
- Objective 4.2c: Demonstrate knowledge of guide properties.
- Objective 4.2d: Demonstrate knowledge of how to change the measurement unit on rulers.
- Objective 4.3a: Demonstrate knowledge of how to change the canvas size.
- Objective 4.3b: Demonstrate knowledge of how to rotate, flip, and straighten an image and how to rotate a canvas

- Topic B
  - Objective 4.1b: Demonstrate knowledge of saving, loading, and editing selections.
- Topic C
  - Objective 4.1d: Demonstrate knowledge of selection commands and how to modify selections.
  - Objective 4.1b: Demonstrate knowledge of saving, loading, and editing selections.
  - Objective 4.1e: Identify when to use feathering and anti-aliasing when making selections.
- Topic D
  - Objective 4.4e: Demonstrate knowledge of how to match, mix, and replace color by using a specific set of tools.
  - Objective 4.6c: Identify tools that are used for painting.
  - Objective 4.6d: Identify tools that are used for drawing or creating shapes.

This lesson covers all or part of the following Adobe Photoshop CS5 ACE Exam objectives:

- Topic A
  - Objective 1.1 Given a scenario, create a selection using an appropriate tool or method.
  - Objective 1.3 Move and transform selections.
  - Objective 2.5 Given a scenario, combine images to make a collage (options include dragging and dropping a closed file into an open document, dragging layers from one open image to another, using Shift to register layers, Paste in Place and Paste Into commands).
  - Objective 9.6 Given a scenario, properly resize an image (options include Image Size dialog box, resampling controls, Canvas Size dialog box, Transform options, Crop tool, and Content Aware Scale).
- Topic B
  - Objective 1.2 Save and load selections.
- Topic C
  - Objective 1.4 Given a scenario, use Refine Edge controls to capture detail in soft and hard selection edges (options include decontaminating edge color).
- Topic D
  - Objective 8.1 Given a scenario, use the Mixer brush and its options properly.
  - Objective 8.3 Given a scenario, choose and use the proper method of choosing a color (options include HUD Color Picker, Eyedropper tool with color ring, Swatches panel, Color panel, and the Color Picker).

TOPIC A
Create a Selection

You determined the image resolution and graphic types. Now, you want to begin working with images. In this topic, you will select and enhance image areas using the various Photoshop tools.

While working with images, you may find it necessary to modify certain portions of an image to enhance it. This requires a careful selection. The built-in tools in Photoshop allow you to make complex selections easily and quickly.

The New Dialog Box

The **New** dialog box is displayed every time you create a document. You can name the document, choose a preset size, or specify the width, height, resolution, and color mode for the document. You can also specify the color of the background contents and specify advanced settings such as color profile and pixel aspect ratio.

The File Information Box

After you create a document, the status bar of the document window displays the file information box. The file information box allows you to view and check the size of the document. The data displayed on the status bar is separated by a slash. The data on the left side of the slash represents the size of the document. The data on the right side of the slash displays the size of the image as Photoshop saves it. This size includes both layers and channels.

The INFO Panel

The **INFO** panel not only provides information about the current document size but also displays information related to the currently selected tool. The color values of the current color mode appear on the left side of the **INFO** panel and the CMYK values appear on the right.

The Marquee Tools

The Marquee tools available in Photoshop allow you to select geometric areas in images. The selections that are made can be moved, transformed, and modified to suit your needs.

Tool	Used To
Rectangular Marquee	Select geometric areas such as boxes.
Elliptical Marquee	Select geometric areas such as circles, ovals, or ellipses.
Single Row Marquee	Select a row of pixels.
Single Column Marquee	Select a column of pixels.

The Lasso Tools

The Lasso tools are used to select complex areas in an image.

Tool	Used To
Lasso	Make freeform straight-edged selections.
Polygonal Lasso	Create straight-edged segments of a selection border. You can also use it to select areas that are made up of straight lines. You can delete recently drawn straight segments by pressing either **Delete** or **Backspace.**
Magnetic Lasso	Select portions of an image with complex edges that are set against a high-contrast background. It allows you to accurately select image areas that contain many colors. You can delete recently drawn straight segments by pressing either **Delete** or **Backspace.**

The Magnetic Lasso Tool Options Bar

The **Magnetic Lasso** tool Options bar contains options that help you in making complex selections more accurate.

Component	Allows You To
Feather text box	Specify the softness of the resulting edges when a selection is completed.
Anti-alias check box	Specify whether the selected area will be anti-aliased.
Width text box	Specify the value that detects the selection edges in pixels.
Contrast text box	Specify a value that enables the **Magnetic Lasso** tool to detect the edges in an image.
Frequency text box	Specify how often the **Magnetic Lasso** tool places snap points on the edges of the selection.

Anti-Aliasing

Anti-aliasing is a feature that allows you to smooth jagged edges by placing light pixels around a selected object. It is often used on text to create the illusion of smooth curves.

The Quick Selection Tool

The *Quick Selection* tool is used to make accurate selections of complex shapes using an adjustable brush tip. When you drag the brush, the selected area expands along the defined edges of the image.

Auto-Enhance

The **Auto-Enhance** option is displayed on the **Quick Selection** tool Options bar. This option is used to automatically select the borders of an image you intend to select. The brush tip is adjusted when it is placed on the border of the image, ensuring a refined and smooth selection without any background pixels.

The Magic Wand Tool

The *Magic Wand* tool is used for selecting pixels of an image that are similar in color or brightness with a single click. You can use this tool to select contiguous or noncontiguous pixels by using the **Contiguous** check box on the Options bar.

The Tolerance Option

The **Tolerance** option allows you to specify the **Magic Wand** tool's sensitivity to color differences. In Photoshop, each pixel within an image is coded with color and brightness information. While using the **Magic Wand** tool, you can specify the range or tolerance of pixels selected to ensure that only pixels similar in color to the pixel you clicked are selected. If the tolerance is low, it means that the tool has less tolerance for color differences and vice versa. The higher the tolerance, the larger the area that the **Magic Wand** tool will select; the lower the tolerance, the smaller the area that the tool will select. You can accurately select the required areas with the **Magic Wand** tool by clicking a color that is in the middle of the tonal range you wish to select. Therefore, it is better to select a color that is lighter than some of the required colors, but darker than the others.

Rulers

In Photoshop, there are two rulers available—the document ruler and the **Ruler** tool. The document ruler is used to position elements or images appropriately. When enabled, the document rulers will appear on the top and left margins of the Photoshop interface. Markers in the rulers show the mouse pointer's position when the mouse pointer is moved.

The **Ruler** tool is a rectangular measuring device that is used to measure the length of an object and draw straight lines. The edges of a ruler are straight, and it has measurements marked on it from start to end. The ruler can be used to draw lines vertically, horizontally, and diagonally.

The Ruler Tool Options Bar

The **Ruler** tool Options bar displays information such as starting and ending points, horizontal and vertical points, and the angle relative to the axis of an object. The **Straighten** button on the Options bar allows you to rotate, scale, and crop an image to fit the canvas. The **Clear** button is used to delete the line drawn.

Guides

A *guide* is a reference line that is used to align objects at particular locations on the canvas. A guide is especially useful for aligning the horizontal and vertical guides to the exact numerical values required. Guides can be colored, moved, locked, and hidden, and also snapped. Nevertheless, they will not be visible when the artwork is printed. Additionally, you can set guide properties such as color and style using the options in the **Preferences** dialog box.

Snapping

Snapping helps align objects precisely on the canvas. You can set snapping to guides, grids, objects on the canvas, slices, pixels, and edges of the document. You can enable snapping for all these components by choosing **View→Snap To→All** and disable snapping by choosing **View→Snap To→None**.

How to Create a Selection

Procedure Reference: Create a Document

To create a document:

1. Choose **File→New.**
2. In the **New** dialog box, specify the desired settings.
   - In the **Name** text box, type a name for the document.
   - From the **Presets** drop-down list, select the size for the document.
   - In the **Width** text box, specify the desired width for the document.
   - In the **Height** text box, specify the desired height for the document.
   - In the **Resolution** text box, specify the desired resolution for the document.
   - From the **Color Mode** drop-down list, select the desired color mode.
   - From the **Background Contents** drop-down list, select the desired background for the document.
3. If necessary, specify the advanced settings.
   - From the **Color Profile** drop-down list, select a profile for the file.
   - From the **Pixel Aspect Ratio** drop-down list, specify the desired pixel aspect ratio for the file.
4. If necessary, click the **Save Preset** button to save the specified settings as presets.
5. Click **OK** to open a document.
6. Save a Photoshop file.
   a. Choose **File→Save.**
   b. If necessary, navigate to the location where you want to save the file.
   c. In the **Save** dialog box, in the **File name** text box, type a name.
   d. From the **Format** drop-down list, select a file format.
   e. Click **Save.**

 To save a copy of a file, choose **File→Save As** and save the file in a different name.

Procedure Reference: Open a Document in Photoshop

To open a document in Photoshop:

1. Open a document.
   a. Choose the desired command to open a document.
      - Choose **File→Open.**

- Choose **File→Open As.**

b.   In the dialog box, navigate to the folder where the file is located.

c.   If necessary, from the **Files of type** drop-down list, select a file format to display files of the selected format.

d.   Select a file.

e.   Click **Open.**

 You can open recent files by choosing **File→Open Recent** and then choosing a recently opened file.

2.   Close the document.

- Choose **File→Close** or;
- On the right corner of the document tab, click the close button.

3.   If necessary, close multiple documents.

a.   Choose **File→Close All.**

b.   In the **Adobe Photoshop CS5 Extended** message box, click the desired button.

- Click **Yes** to save the document and close it.
- Click **No** to close the document without saving it.
- Click **Cancel** to stop the closing action.

 The **Adobe Photoshop CS5 Extended** message box is displayed for every document that is opened.

Procedure Reference: Modify the Canvas Size

To modify the canvas size:

1.   Choose **Image→Canvas Size.**

2.   In the **Canvas Size** dialog box, specify the dimensions of the canvas.

- Check the **Relative** check box to specify the increase and decrease in canvas size.
- In the **New Size** section, from the drop-down list next to the **Width** text box, select a unit of measurement.
- In the **Width** text box, type a value.
- In the **Height** text box, type a value.

3.   If necessary, in the **Anchor** section, specify the direction in which the canvas is to be modified.

4.   If necessary, from the **Canvas extension color** drop-down list, select an option to set the background color.

5.   Click **OK.**

Procedure Reference: Create a Selection

To create a selection:

1.   Open the document in which you want to create a selection.

2. Make a selection.

- Make a rectangular selection.
    a. In the **Tools** panel, select the **Rectangular Marquee** tool.
    b. Position the cross hair mouse pointer at the location where you want to start the selection, and drag to make a rectangular marquee selection.
    c. If necessary, continue to hold down the mouse button and press the **Spacebar** to move the selection as you draw it.

 You may want to move the selection marquee if the area you selected is approximately the right size but is not centered over the pixels you wished to select.

- Make an elliptical selection.
    a. Select the **Elliptical Marquee** tool.
        - Click and hold the **Rectangular Marquee** tool, and from the flyout, select the **Elliptical Marquee** tool or;
        - Right-click the **Rectangular Marquee** tool, and from the flyout, select the **Elliptical Marquee** tool.
    b. Position the cross hair mouse pointer at the location where you want to start the selection, and drag to make an elliptical marquee selection.
- Make a freehand selection.
    a. Select a Lasso tool.
    b. Click at the outer edge of the object or on the portion of the image to be selected, and drag to make a freehand selection.
    c. Release the mouse button to end the selection at the same location where it was started.
- Make a selection based on color.
    a. Select the **Magic Wand** tool.
    b. On the Options bar, specify the desired settings.
    c. In the image, click the color you want to select.
- Make a quick selection.
    a. Click and hold the **Magic Wand** tool, and from the flyout, select the **Quick Selection** tool.
    b. Position the cross hair mouse pointer at the location where you want to start the selection, and drag to make a quick selection of the image.

3. If necessary, delete the selected area of the image.
- Choose **Edit→Clear** or;
- Press **Delete** or;
- Press **Backspace.**

4. If necessary, remove the selection.
- Choose **Select→Deselect** or;
- Press **Ctrl+D.**

If necessary, press **Caps Lock** to display the cross hair mouse pointer instead of the tool mouse pointer for creating more accurate selections, and then click and drag to make the selection.

Selection Commands

There are a number of commands available on the **Select** menu, which can be used to work with selections.

Command	Used To
All	Select all pixels on a selected layer.
Deselect	Deselect a selection.
Reselect	Select the most recent selection.
Inverse	Reverse the selection.

Procedure Reference: Move, Copy, and Paste a Selection

To move, copy, and paste a selection:

1. Select a portion of an image using any selection tool.
2. Move the selection to a different location within a document or outside the document.
    a. In the **Tools** panel, select the **Move** tool.
    b. Click anywhere inside the selection and drag it to the desired location.
3. If necessary, move the selection using any selection tool.
4. Copy a selection.
    - Choose **Edit→Copy** to copy the selection or;
    - Choose **Edit→Copy Merged** to merge the copy of all layers in the selected area.
5. Paste a selection.
    - Choose **Edit→Paste** to paste the selection.
    - Choose **Edit→Paste Special→Paste In Place** to paste the selection in the same selected location.
    - Choose **Edit→Paste Special→Paste Into** to paste the selection along with the copied selection in the same location.
    - Choose **Edit→Paste Special→Paste Outside** to paste the selection around the selection.

Deselection

When you want to remove a selection, choose the **Deselect** command on the **Select** menu. You can also click inside a selection using selection tools such as **Marquee, Lasso,** and **Magic Wand** to deselect a selection. Unlike with other graphic applications, clicking a blank space to deselect a selection is not possible in Photoshop. Because the entire image is made up of individual pixels, there is no empty or transparent space in a Photoshop image unless you add layers. White space in a single-layer image is simply a large area of white pixels.

Procedure Reference: Select from Center Toward the Edges

To select from center toward the edges:

 It is often difficult to estimate where to begin dragging an elliptical marquee in order to enclose an entire object perfectly. However, you can select from the center of an object toward the edge, instead of from the edge, to simplify selections.

1. Select a marquee tool.
2. Position the mouse pointer at the center of the object to be selected.
3. Click at the center, press **Alt+Shift,** and drag to constrain a shape, and draw a selection from the center toward the edge.
4. When the selection matches the object, complete the selection by first releasing the mouse button and then releasing the **Alt** and **Shift** keys.

Procedure Reference: Crop the Extra Space Around the Edges

To crop the extra space around the edges:

1. Crop an image using the **Crop** tool.
   a. In the **Tools** panel, select the **Crop** tool.
   b. Drag a crop marquee to enclose the entire image.
   c. Crop the extra space.
      - Drag a crop handle near the edge of the image until the crop marquee snaps itself to the edge by default or;
      - Hold down **Ctrl** and drag the crop handle near the edge of the image to position the marquee precisely on the edge.
   d. Press **Enter** to crop the unwanted space around the edges of the image.
2. Crop an image using the **Crop** command.
   a. In the **Tools** panel, select the **Crop** tool.
   b. Crop the extra space.
      - Drag a crop handle near the edge of the image until the crop marquee snaps itself to the edge by default or;
      - Hold down **Ctrl** and drag the crop handle near the edge of the image to position the marquee precisely on the edge.
   c. Choose **Image→Crop.**
3. Crop an image using the **Trim** command.
   a. Choose **Image→Trim.**
   b. In the **Trim** dialog box, specify the desired option.
   c. Click **OK.**

Differences Between Resampling and Cropping

While resampling allows you to resize the image by reducing the resolution of the image, cropping allows you to resize the image by trimming off the transparent edges around the image.

Procedure Reference: Modify the Image Using the Ruler Tool

To modify the image using the **Ruler** tool:

1. Open a document in Photoshop.
2. In the **Tools** panel, select the **Ruler** tool.
3. Click at a point from where you want to start and click at the point where you want to end the line.
4. If necessary, on the Options bar, click the **Clear** button to delete the drawn line.
5. On the Options bar, click the **Straighten** button.

Procedure Reference: Set Preferences for Rulers

To set preferences for rulers:

1. Display the **Preferences** dialog box.
   - Choose **Edit→Preferences→General** and in the **Preferences** dialog box, in the left pane, select **Units & Rulers** or;
   - Choose **Edit→Preferences→Units & Rulers.**
2. Set preferences for rulers.
   - In the **Units** section, select the desired option.
     - From the **Rulers** drop-down list, select an option.
     - From the **Type** drop-down list, select an option.
   - In the **Column Size** section, select the desired option.
     - In the **Width** text box, double-click and select the value or type a value.
     - From the **Points** drop-down list, select an option.
     - In the **Gutter** text box, double-click and select the value or type a value.
     - From the **Points** drop-down list, select an option.
   - In the **New Document Preset Resolutions** section, specify the desired settings.
     - In the **Print Resolution** text box, select the value and type a new value.
     - From the **Pixels/inch** drop-down list, select an option.
     - In the **Screen Resolution** text box, select the value and type a new value.
     - From the **Pixels/inch** drop-down list, select an option.
3. Click **OK.**
4. If necessary, choose **View→Rulers** to show or hide the rulers.

Procedure Reference: Add Guides

To add guides:

1. Choose **View→Rulers.**
2. Add guides.
   a. Choose **View→New Guide.**
   b. In the **New Guide** dialog box, in the **Orientation** section, select an option.
      - Select the **Horizontal** option to display rulers horizontally.

- Select the **Vertical** option to display rulers vertically.

   c.   In the **Position** text box, type a value.

   d.   Click **OK.**

   e.   Click the horizontal or vertical ruler and drag to add a horizontal or vertical guide.

3.   If necessary, choose **View→Lock Guides** to fix the guides in the same position.

4.   If necessary, remove guides.

- Choose **View→Show→Guides** to hide guides or;
- Choose **View→Clear→Guides** to remove guides or;
- Click the horizontal or vertical guide and drag it to the respective ruler away from the workspace.

5.   If necessary, enable snapping to guides.

- Choose **View→Snap** to enable snapping.
- Choose **View→Snap To** to enable snapping for particular components such as guides, grids, layers, and so on.

Procedure Reference: Work with the MINI BRIDGE Panel

To work with the **MINI BRIDGE** panel:

1.   Launch the **MINI BRIDGE** panel.

- On the Application bar, click the **Launch Mini Bridge** button or;
- Choose **File→Browse in Mini Bridge.**

2.   Click the **Go to parent, recent items, or Favorites** button to navigate to files or folders.

3.   If necessary, in the **MINI BRIDGE** panel, click the **Go to Adobe Bridge** button to launch the Bridge application.

4.   From the **Panel View** drop-down menu, choose a command to display the menus and pods.

5.   Click the **Search** button to search for the stored files.

ACTIVITY 4-1
Creating a Selection

Data Files:

Home Resized.psd

Scenario:

The support files for the color sample card have been created by members of your design team. You need to place some of these images on the outer page of the card, and will begin by importing them into Photoshop. You then want to transfer the images onto a new document and work on them, independent of the other project files.

---

1. Create a document named ***Color Sample Card.***

   a. Choose **File→New.**

   b. In the **New** dialog box, in the **Name** text box, type ***Color Sample Card***

   c. In the **Resolution** text box, double-click and type ***200***

   d. From the **Width** drop-down list, select **pixels.**

   e. In the **Width** text box, double-click and type ***5600***

   f. In the **Height** text box, double-click and type ***2800***

   g. From the **Background Contents** drop-down list, select **Transparent** and click **OK.**

---

2. Transfer the home image to the new document to create a front page for the color sample card.

   a. Choose **File→Open.**

   b. In the **Open** dialog box, navigate to the C:\084384Data\Working with Selections folder and open the Home Resized.psd file.

   c. Choose **Window→Arrange→Float in Window.**

   d. In the **Tools** panel, select the **Move** tool.

   e. Click anywhere on the home image and drag it onto the new document.

   f. Close the Home Resized.psd file.

   g. On the status bar, in the magnification text box, double-click, type ***18*** and then press **Enter.**

   h. Choose **View→Rulers.**

   i. Click the vertical ruler and drag the guide to the 1400-pixel mark on the horizontal ruler.

j.   Position the home image so that the top-left corner of the image is placed at the intersection of the 1400-pixel mark on the horizontal ruler and the 0-pixel mark on the vertical ruler.

3.   Transfer the blue can image onto the color sample card.

    a.   Choose **File→Open** navigate to the C:\084384Data\Working with Selections folder, and open the Blue Paint Can.jpg file.

    b.   Choose **Window→Arrange→Float in Window** to display it as a separate window.

    c.   Place the Blue Paint Can window to the right of the interface so that the empty space to the left of the home image is visible.

    d.   Click the blue paint can image and drag it to the Color Sample Card document.

    e.   Close the Blue Paint Can.jpg file.

    f.   Click the horizontal ruler and drag the guide to the 2000-pixel mark on the vertical ruler.

    g.   Scroll to the left of the document.

    h.   Click the vertical ruler and drag the guide to the 150-pixel mark on the horizontal ruler.

    i.   Click the paint can image and drag it to the point of intersection of the 150-pixel mark on the horizontal ruler and the 2000-pixel mark on the vertical ruler to position the blue paint can image.

4.   Select the white background in the paint can image to delete it.

    a.   On the status bar, in the magnification text box, double-click, type *70* and then press **Enter.**

    b.   In the **NAVIGATOR** panel, drag the red outline to the blue paint can image to view it.

    c.   In the **Tools** panel, from the **Quick Selection** tool flyout, select the **Magic Wand** tool.

    d.   On the Options bar, in the **Tolerance** text box, double-click, type *2* and then press **Enter.**

    e.   Click anywhere in the white space around the paint can.

5.   Save the document.

    a.   Choose **File→Save.**

    b.   In the **Save As** dialog box, verify that in the **File name** text box, **Color Sample Card.psd** is displayed and click **Save.**

    c.   In the **Photoshop Format Options** message box, check the **Don't show again** check box and click **OK.**

ACTIVITY 4-2
Making a Selection

Data Files:

Flower.psd

Before You Begin:

Navigate to the C:\084384Data\Working with Selections folder and open the Flower.psd file.

Scenario:

In addition to the color sample card, you need to create a brochure modeling the interior of a room. You need decorative items like flower vase suitable to the interior design. You found a suitable flower vase image from the library. But, you need to remove the background from the image, so that the image can be transferred to the interior design file.

1. Select the white background around the flower vase image to delete it.

   a. In the **Tools** panel, verify that the **Magic Wand** tool is selected.

   b. On the Options bar, in the **Tolerance** text box, double-click, type *32* and then press **Enter.**

   c. Click the white space around the flower vase image to select the white background.

   d. Press **Delete** to delete the selection.

   e. Choose **Select→Deselect** to deselect the selection.

   f. On the status bar, in the magnification text box, double-click, type *18* and then press **Enter.**

g. Observe that there are still some white patches between the flowers.

h. Click at the point of intersection of the 2800-pixel mark on the horizontal ruler and the 3000-pixel mark on the vertical ruler to select the white portion between the flowers.

i. On the Options bar, click the **Add to Selection** button.

j. Click at the point of intersection of the 1400-pixel mark on the horizontal ruler and the 4200-pixel mark on the vertical ruler to select the white portion between the flowers.

k. Similarly, select the rest of the white spaces found between the flowers.

 To make proper selection and avoid selecting neighboring pixels, you can increase the zoom percentage and then select the white space.

l. Press **Delete** to delete the selection.

m. Choose **Select→Deselect** to deselect the selection.

n. On the status bar, in the magnification text box, double-click, type *12* and then press **Enter.**

2. Save the file.

a. Choose **File→Save As.**

b. In the **Save As** dialog box, in the **File name** text box, type *My Flower* and click **Save.**

TOPIC B
Save a Selection

You selected specific areas of an image using the selection tools. You may want to use these selections in the future for different purposes. In this topic, you will save the selections you made.

When working with images, you may find that you have to make complex selections. Once you complete the task, you probably do not want to repeat it. Photoshop allows you to save the selections you made with specific names.

Channels

A *channel* is a grayscale image that contains unique information about the image in Photoshop. Photoshop uses channels to divide color images into components. For example, RGB images are divided into red, green, and blue channels. Non-color images such as grayscale and black and white need only one channel because the colors need not be divided into components.

The Alpha Channel

Alpha channel is a channel that appears in the **CHANNELS** panel when you save a selection. It allows you to store the transparency information of the images in a file without affecting the color channels.

Alpha Channel vs. Color Channel

Every Photoshop image contains one or more color channels that stores information about the colors in the image. The default color channels vary according to the color mode of the image. For example, an RGB image has a separate channel for each color Red, Green, and Blue. In addition to this, it also has a composite channel that is used to edit an image. Alpha channels store image selections in the grayscale mode. They can be added to create masks to either manipulate or protect certain image areas. Alpha channels are preserved only when an image file is saved either in the PDF, TIFF, raw, or PSB formats.

The CHANNELS Panel

The **CHANNELS** panel lists all the channels used in the current image. The list includes a thumbnail of the channel contents along with the channel name. When you edit a channel, it will be updated automatically in the panel. You can change the channel visibility to show or hide the channel. Additionally, you can create, duplicate, delete, split, and merge channels, and change the size of the thumbnails using the panel menu options available in the panel.

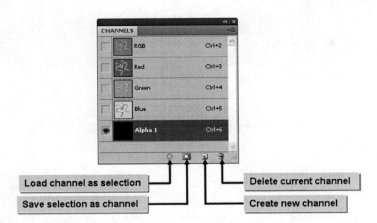

Figure 4-1: An alpha channel displayed in the CHANNELS panel.

How to Save a Selection

Procedure Reference: Save a Selection

To save a selection:

1. Create a selection using a selection tool.
2. Choose **Select→Save Selection.**
3. In the **Save Selection** dialog box, in the **Destination** section, specify the desired settings.
   a. From the **Document** drop-down list, select the file to be used as a source.

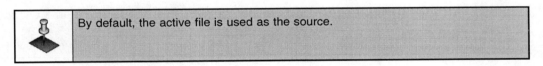
By default, the active file is used as the source.

   b. In the **Name** text box, specify a name for the selection and click **OK.**
4. If necessary, choose **Select→Deselect** to deselect the selection.

Procedure Reference: Rename a Saved Selection

To rename a saved selection:

1. Choose **Window→Channels** to display the **CHANNELS** panel.
2. Double-click the alpha channel.
3. In the **Channel Options** dialog box, in the **Name** text box, type a different name and click **OK.**
4. If necessary, click the **Indicates channel visibility** icon to view or hide the channel.

ACTIVITY 4-3
Saving a Selection

Data Files:

Color Sample Card.psd, Blue Paint Can.jpg

Before You Begin:

Switch to the Color Sample Card.psd file.

Scenario:

You need to import similar images onto your color sample card. Because the images require identical modifications, you decide to save a selection to save time by eliminating unnecessary rework.

1. Save the selection.

    a. Choose **Select→Save Selection.**

    b. In the **Save Selection** dialog box, in the **Destination** section, in the **Name** text box, type *Can* and click **OK.**

    c. Choose **Select→Deselect.**

    d. Select the **CHANNELS** panel.

    e. In the **CHANNELS** panel, observe that the **Can** selection is saved as a channel.

    f. Save the file.

2. **Which statement is correct with regard to the CHANNELS panel options menu?**

    a) You can create, delete, split, and merge channels but cannot duplicate channels using the CHANNELS panel options menu.

    b) You can create, duplicate, delete, split, and merge channels, but cannot change the size of the thumbnails using the CHANNELS panel options menu.

    c) You can create, duplicate, delete, split, and merge channels, and change the size of the thumbnails using the CHANNELS panel options menu.

    d) You cannot change the size of the thumbnails using the CHANNELS panel options menu.

TOPIC C
Modify a Selection

You saved the selected areas of an image. However, you can enhance a selection by adding new areas to it or by deleting existing areas from it. In this topic, you will modify a selection.

Selecting image areas accurately is a difficult task, especially when making complex selections, which is time consuming and taxing. Moreover, you just need to slightly modify the selection to make an accurate selection, but while doing so, you may collapse the entire selection. By using various options and features available in Photoshop, making complex selections becomes much more easier and quicker.

The Refine Edge Dialog Box

The **Refine Edge** dialog box contains various options that allow you to improve the quality of the edges of a selection by increasing the selection area, sharpening the edges, and reducing irregular areas. You can create soft-edged transitions and shrink or enlarge the selection boundary. In addition to that, you can remove the influence of colors along the selection edges on the selected pixels by using the **Decontaminate Colors** option and you can edit the selection by viewing it against backgrounds such as **Marching Ants, Overlay, On Black, On White, Black & White, On Layers,** and **Reveal Layer.**

The **Refine Edge** dialog box also provides access to the **Zoom** and **Hand** tools, and has two additional tools—the **Refine Radius** and **Erase Refinements** tools, which can be used to make selections more accurately.

The Feather Effect

Feathering allows you to create a blurred transition between the selection edge and the surrounding pixels, and specify the width of the feathered edge. Feathering does not change the colors of pixels. Instead, it reduces the opacity over the specified feather area. The Feather effect is applied to the selection only when you move, cut, or fill the feathered selection.

Feather Effects in a Selection

Feathering can be used to create a variety of effects such as silhouetting. You can specify the pixel value for the feather using the **Feather** text box on the Options bar. This value can be specified for selections created using the **Marquee** and **Lasso** tools. The value must be entered before making the selection, or it will have no effect. If you want to add a feather effect to an existing selection, you must use the **Feather** command on the **Select** menu.

How to Modify a Selection

Procedure Reference: Load a Selection

To load a selection:

1. Save a selection.
2. Choose **Select→Load Selection.**
3. In the **Load Selection** dialog box, from the **Channel** drop-down list, select the channel containing the saved selection.
4. Click **OK.**

Procedure Reference: Modify a Selection Manually

To modify a selection manually:

1. Create a selection using a selection tool.
2. On the Options bar, click a button to modify the selection.
   - Click the **New selection** button to select new areas.
   - Click the **Add to selection** button to add new areas to an existing selection.
   - Click the **Subtract from selection** button to deselect parts of an existing selection.
   - Click the **Intersect with selection** button to create a selection that intersects with the existing selection.
3. Click and drag the mouse pointer over the existing selection to modify it.
4. If necessary, save the selection.

Procedure Reference: Modify a Selection Using Menu Commands

To modify a selection using menu commands:

1. Create a selection using a selection tool.
2. Choose the desired command to modify a selection.
   - Choose **Select→Modify→Border** to specify the value for the border width.
   - Choose **Select→Modify→Smooth** to smoothen the edges of the selection.
   - Choose **Select→Modify→Expand** to expand the selection.
   - Choose **Select→Modify→Contract** to contract the selection.
   - Choose **Select→Modify→Feather** to feather the selection.
3. In the dialog box, specify the number of pixels.
4. Click **OK.**

Procedure Reference: Refine the Edges of a Selection

To refine the edges of a selection:

1. Make a selection.
2. On the Options bar, click **Refine Edge.**
3. In the **Refine Edge** dialog box, specify the desired settings such as view mode, smoothness, feathering, contrast, applying smart radius, and more.
4. Click **OK.**

ACTIVITY 4-4
Modifying the Paint Can Selection

Data Files:

Color Sample Card.psd, Green Paint Can.jpg

Before You Begin:

1. Navigate to the C:\084384Data\Working with Selections folder and open the Green Paint Can.jpg file.
2. Display the Color Sample Card.psd file.

Scenario:

The edges of the selection you have been working on look sharp and there is also some white space on the image. You would like to remove the excess space to correct the imperfection. An experienced coworker tells you that you can smooth the edges to remove the imperfections and lend a more esthetic appeal to the image. But before correcting the saved selection, you apply the selection to the same image and after the correction, reuse it to other similar images.

---

1. Load the selection and modify it to make an accurate selection.

    a. Set the zoom percentage of the document to **300**

    b. Choose **Select→Load Selection** to load the previously saved selection.

    c. In the **Load Selection** dialog box, in the **Source** section, from the **Channel** drop-down list, select **Can** and click **OK.**

    d. In the **NAVIGATOR** panel, drag the red navigation box over the blue paint can image to view the right handle of the can.

    e. Observe that the white space inside the handle has not been selected.

    f. On the Options bar, verify that the **Add to Selection** button, is selected and click the white space inside the right handle to select that area.

    g. In the document, scroll to the left to view the left handle of the paint can.

    h. Click the white space inside the left handle to select that area.

    i. Press **Delete** to delete the white space in the image.

      j.   Set the zoom percentage to *18*

      k.   In the **NAVIGATOR** panel, click the red outline to view the images in the document.

2.   Save the modified selection.

      a.   Choose **Select→Save Selection.**

      b.   In the **Save Selection** dialog box, in the **Destination** section, from the **Channel** drop-down list, select **Can.**

      c.   In the **Operation** section, select the **Add to Channel** option and click **OK.**

      d.   Choose **Select→Deselect.**

3.   Transfer the green paint can image to the workspace and load the selection.

      a.   Move the green paint can onto the Color Sample Card document.

      b.   Close the Green Paint Can.jpg file.

      c.   Select the **CHANNELS** panel.

      d.   In the **CHANNELS** panel, for the **Can** channel, click in the **Indicates channel visibility** column to display the channel.

      e.   Drag the green paint can to fit within the loaded selection.

      f.   Choose **Select→Load Selection.**

      g.   From the **Channel** drop-down list, select **Can** and click **OK.**

      h.   Press **Delete.**

      i.   Choose **Select→Deselect.**

      j.   In the **CHANNELS** panel, for the **Can** channel, click in the **Indicates channel visibility** column to hide the channel.

      k.   Drag the green paint can and place it to the right of the blue paint can.

      l.   Save the file.

ACTIVITY 4-5
Modifying the Flower Vase Selection

Data Files:

My Flower.psd

Setup:

Display the My Flower.psd file.

Scenario:

You feel that the selection you made on the flower vase has some imperfections, especially on the edges. So, you decide to modify the edges of the selection to make it smooth and fine to get a proper selection.

---

1. Modify the jagged edges of the flower vase.

   a. In the **Tools** panel, select the **Magic Wand** tool and click in the transparent background that is around the flower vase.

   b. On the status bar, in the magnification text box, double-click, type **150** and then press **Enter.**

   c. Select the **NAVIGATOR** panel, and in that panel click and drag the red outline to the left bottom of the vase.

   d. Observe that there are jagged edges that need to be modified to make a smooth selection.

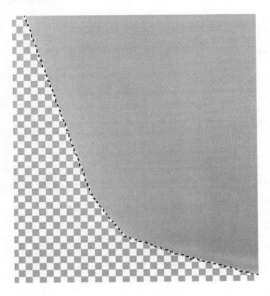

   e. On the Options bar, click **Refine Edge** to display the **Refine Edge** dialog box.

   f. In the **View Mode** section, click the **View** drop-down arrow and select **Black & White (K)** to view the selected area in black and white mode.

g. Click the **View** drop-down arrow again to hide the drop-down list.

h. In the **Edge Detection** section, in the **Radius** text box, type *1* and press **Tab.**

i. In the **Adjust Edge** section, in the **Smooth** text box, type *4* and press **Tab.**

j. Specify the values for **Feather** and **Contrast** as *1* and *2,* respectively.

k. Press **OK.**

2. Remove the jagged portion of the selection and save the file.

a. Press **Delete** to delete the selection and set the zoom percentage to *12*

b. Choose **Select→Deselect.**

c. Save and close the file.

TOPIC D
Apply Color to a Selection

You modified selections. After having finalized the selections, you may want to apply color to the selections. In this topic, you will apply color to selections in a document.

When working with images, you may often find that the color applied to a particular area of an image is not appropriate or it needs to be retouched. Retouching those specific areas of an image will add more esthetic appeal to it. Photoshop offers several tools for applying colors to selections.

Painting Tools

Photoshop includes a wide variety of painting tools that allow you to apply and modify colors in an image.

The following table describes some of the painting tools.

Tool	Allows You To
Brush	Apply foreground color when you drag the mouse pointer within an image. It creates freehand lines that can have soft or hard edges.
Pencil	Apply foreground color when you drag the mouse pointer within an image. It creates freehand lines that always have hard edges.
Color Replacement	Replace the selected color with a new color.
Mixer Brush	Create natural and realistic painting effects. It allows you to blend colors with the underlying colors in an image.
Eraser	Erase pixels in an image.
Gradient	Apply a blend of multiple colors. You can either use preset gradients or create a gradient.
Paint Bucket	Fill the neighboring pixels that have similar color values with the selected color or pattern.
Art History Brush	Paint on an image with a stylized stroke using the data from a previous history state.

The Eyedropper Tool

The **Eyedropper** tool allows you to pick a foreground or background color by sampling the existing colors from an image. You can select colors from any of the open images, the **COLOR** panel, or the **SWATCHES** panel. You can also pick colors from outside the application.

The Color Picker Dialog Box

The **Color Picker** dialog box allows you to select the foreground and background colors. The colors displayed here are based on four color modes—HSB, RGB, Lab, and CMYK. You can either select a color from the color field or enter numeric values of the color.

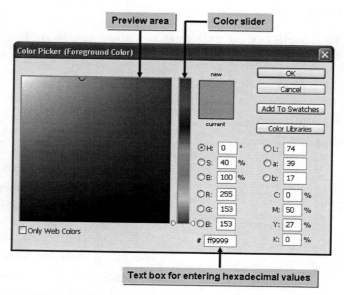

Figure 4-2: The Color Picker dialog box with its various options displayed.

Hexadecimal Color System

The hexadecimal color system consists of six digits. The hexadecimal code can be broken into three separate groups—the Red, Green, and Blue color values. Each digit is a value from 0 to F, in the hexadecimal system. The hexadecimal color system counts by 0 1 2 3 4 5 6 7 8 9 A B C D E F, with 0 being the null value and F being the highest value.

How to Apply Color to a Selection

Procedure Reference: Select a Foreground Color

To select a foreground color:

1. Open the required Photoshop file.
2. Select a foreground color.
   - In the **Tools** panel, click the **Set Foreground Color** icon and in the **Color Picker** dialog box, drag the slider in the color ramp to select the desired color or;
   - In the **COLOR** panel, click the **Set Foreground Color** icon and from the color ramp at the bottom of the panel, select the desired color or;
   - In the **COLOR** panel, click the **Set Foreground Color** icon and drag the Red, Green, and Blue color sliders or specify values in their respective text boxes to set the desired color or;
   - Select the **Eyedropper** tool and click the desired foreground color within the image or;
   - In the **SWATCHES** panel, click the desired color.

 Certain swatches can be saved by clicking the **Add To Swatches** button in the **Color Picker** dialog box and then by giving them a name.

Procedure Reference: Select a Background Color

To select a background color:

1. Open the required Photoshop file.
2. Select a background color.
   - In the **Tools** panel, click the **Set Background Color** icon and in the **Color Picker** dialog box, drag the slider in the color ramp to select the desired color or;
   - In the **COLOR** panel, click the **Background Color** icon and from the color ramp at the bottom of the panel, select the desired color or;
   - In the **COLOR** panel, click the **Background Color** icon and drag the Red, Green, and Blue color sliders, or specify the values in their respective text boxes to set the desired color or;
   - Select the **Eyedropper** tool, hold down **Alt,** and click the desired background color within the image or;
   - In the **SWATCHES** panel, hold down **Ctrl,** and click the desired color.

 In addition to picking colors from inside the application, you can also pick colors from outside the application using the **Eyedropper** tool.

Procedure Reference: Fill Color in a Selection

To fill color in a selection:

1. Select a particular area on an image using any selection tool.
2. In the **Tools** panel, select the **Paint Bucket** tool.

3. Click in the selection to apply the desired color to it.

4. Choose **Select→Deselect.**

Procedure Reference: Apply Gradient for a Selection

To apply gradients to a selection:

1. Select a particular area on an image using any selection tool.
2. In the **Tools** panel, select the **Gradient** tool.
3. On the Options bar, select the gradient preset fill.
   a. Click the **Click to open Gradient picker** drop-down list.
   b. Select the desired gradient fill preset.
4. If necessary, on the Options bar, select the desired gradient type.
5. In the selected area of an image, click at the point where you want to start and drag to the point where you want to stop applying a gradient fill.

Procedure Reference: Create a Gradient Fill

To create a gradient fill:

1. In the **Tools** panel, select the **Gradient** tool.
2. Create a gradient fill.
   a. Click the **Click to edit the gradient** gradient bar to display the **Gradient Editor** window.
   b. At the bottom left of the gradient slider, click the **Color Stop** icon.
   c. Display the **Select stop color** dialog box to select the color.
      - In the **Stops** section, click the color box or;
      - Double-click the **Color Stop** button.
   d. Select the desired color and click **OK.**
   e. At the bottom right of the gradient slider, click the **Color Stop** and repeat the steps (c and d) to select the color for the right color stop.
   f. If necessary, set the opacity.
      A. At the top left of the gradient slider, click the **Opacity Stop** icon.
      B. In the **Stops** section, drag the **Change opacity of selected stop** slider or in the **Opacity** text box, type the desired value.
      C. Repeat the steps (A and B) to specify the value for the opacity.
3. If necessary, on the Options bar, select the desired gradient type.
4. In the selected area of an image, click at the point where you want to start and drag to the point where you want to stop applying a gradient fill.

ACTIVITY 4-6
Applying Color

Data Files:

Color Sample Card.psd

Before You Begin:

The Color Sample Card.psd file is open.

Scenario:

You feel that modifying a portion of the image that you imported will enhance the image and complement the cover design of your color sample card. You decide to apply gradients instead of solid colors to the image to increase the esthetic appeal of the design.

---

1. Delete the existing sky background to apply gradient fill.

   a. In the **Tools** panel, select the **Move** tool.

   b. Hold down **Ctrl** and select the home image.

   c. In the **Tools** panel, verify that the **Magic Wand** tool is selected and on the Options bar, in the **Tolerance** text box, verify that the value **32** is displayed.

   d. In the **Tools** panel, select the **Magic Wand** tool and on the Options bar, in the **Tolerance** text box, verify that the value **32** is displayed.

   e. In the sky background of the home image, to the top right of the roof, click to select a part of the sky.

   f. Click the rest of the sky image until the entire sky is selected and press **Delete** to delete the selection.

---

2. Apply gradient color to the selection to enhance the image.

   a. In the **Tools** panel, select the **Gradient** tool.

   b. On the Options bar, click the **Click to edit the gradient** box, [gradient swatch] to display the **Gradient Editor** window.

   c. On the gradient slider, click the **Color Stop** button in the lower left.

   d. In the **Stops** section, click the color box to display the **Select stop color** dialog box.

   e. In the # text box, double-click, type *26609d* and then click **OK.**

   f. On the gradient slider, click the **Color Stop** button in the lower right.

   g. In the **Stops** section, click the color box to display the **Select stop color** dialog box.

   h. In the # text box, double-click, type *6fa6d8* and then click **OK.**

   i. Click **OK** to close the **Gradient Editor** dialog box.

j.   Click at the point of intersection of the 2400-pixel mark on the horizontal ruler and the 100-pixel mark on the vertical ruler, hold down **Shift,** and drag downward to the end of the selection to fill the background.

k.   Choose **Select→Deselect** to deselect the selection, and then save and close the file.

Lesson 4 Follow-up

In this lesson, you worked with selections and applied colors to them. By using the built-in selection tools, you can make complex selections and save them for future use, saving you time and effort. You can add new areas to a selection or eliminate a part before finalizing it. You can also add colors to selections and make images look attractive and realistic.

1.   **Which selection tools do you think will be useful to you in your job? Why?**

2.   **Which painting tool do you think will be used most often in your job?**

5 Working with Layers

Lesson Time: 1 hour(s), 30 minutes

Lesson Objectives:

In this lesson, you will work with multiple layers.

You will:

- Create layers.
- Work with type layers.
- Transform layers.
- Apply styles.
- Undo previous steps.
- Manage layers.

Introduction

You worked with selections and modified them and then saved the images in Adobe® Photoshop® CS5's native format. Sometimes, you may want to work with only specific elements in a graphic. In this lesson, you will work with layers.

Imagine a book with transparent cellophane sheets comprising a basic drawing of the human body. You will be able to understand the anatomy better if each unit is explained separately, and as you keep adding the other transparent sheets, the image of the anatomy is completed. Similarly, in Photoshop, separate layers contain objects or images that are part of your design. Using layers, you can select and manipulate composite images, where every element in an image can be positioned and edited separately.

This lesson covers all or part of the following Adobe Visual Communication using Photoshop CS5 objectives:

- Topic A
  - Objective 3.2a: Identify and label elements of the different types of layers.
  - Objective 3.2d: Demonstrate knowledge of how to edit layers.
  - Objective 3.2h: Demonstrate knowledge of how to nest layers.
  - Objective 3.2i: Demonstrate knowledge of how to add, delete, hide, show, lock, unlock, merge, duplicate, and rename layers.
- Topic B

- ■ Objective 2.3a: Demonstrate knowledge of how background image can affect text.
- ■ Objective 2.3b: Identify an appropriate font size, type, and color for a variety of situations.
- ■ Objective 2.3c: Identify an appropriate placement of text for a variety of situations.
- ■ Objective 4.7a: Demonstrate knowledge of the functionality of each type panel option.
- ■ Objective 4.7b: Demonstrate knowledge of functionality of type tools.
- ■ Objective 4.7c: Demonstrate knowledge of the uses of type layers.
- ■ Objective 4.7d: Demonstrate knowledge of how to edit type.
- ● Topic C
  - ■ Objective 3.1f: Demonstrate knowledge of navigating images, rotating the canvas, and using pan and zoom.
  - ■ Objective 4.3b: Demonstrate knowledge of how to rotate, flip, and straighten an image and how to rotate a canvas.
  - ■ Objective 4.3c: Identify tools that are used to modify shapes.
  - ■ Objective 4.3d: Demonstrate knowledge of how to scale, rotate, or skew a selection.
- ● Topic D
  - ■ Objective 3.2b: Demonstrate knowledge of masks and modes.
  - ■ Objective 4.5f: Identify that blending determines how the pixels on a layer interact with the pixels on the layers below.
  - ■ Objective 4.5g: Demonstrate knowledge of how to use blending tools.
  - ■ Objective 4.5h: Demonstrate knowledge of opacity and fill.
  - ■ Objective 4.5i: Demonstrate knowledge of when to use various blending mode options.
  - ■ Objective 4.8b: Demonstrate knowledge of how to apply and remove layer effects or layer styles.
  - ■ Objective 4.8c: Demonstrate knowledge of how to apply layer styles to type.
- ● Topic E
  - ■ Objective 4.1g: Identify the methods or commands for undoing a selection.
- ● Topic F
  - ■ Objective 3.2e: Demonstrate knowledge of how to create layer groups and links.
  - ■ Objective 3.2f: Demonstrate knowledge of how to flatten layers.
  - ■ Objective 3.2g: Identify the differences between a layered file and a flattened file.

This lesson covers all or part of the following Adobe Photoshop CS5 ACE Exam objectives:
- ● Topic A
  - ■ Objective 1.3 Move and transform selections.
  - ■ Objective 2.1 Create and manage layers in the Layers panel (includes creating, reordering, selecting, controlling visibility of, duplicating, locking, clipping, grouping, deleting layers).
- ● Topic B
  - ■ Objective 4.0 Create and edit type layers.
- ● Topic C

- Objective 1.4 Given a scenario, use Refine Edge controls to capture detail in soft and hard selection edges (options include decontaminating edge color).

- Objective 9.6 Given a scenario, properly resize an image (options include Image Size dialog box, resampling controls, Canvas Size dialog box, Transform options, Crop tool, and Content Aware Scale).

- Objective 9.7 Given a scenario, know how to crop and straighten an image (include grid for rule-of-thirds, perspective cropping, and the Ruler tool Straighten option).

- Topic D
  - Objective 2.2 Given a scenario, use layer Blend modes to achieve a desired effect.

  - Objective 2.3 Given a scenario, use Opacity and Fill controls in the layers panel to achieve a desired effect (options include ability to vary Opacity/fill of multiple layers).

  - Objective 2.6 Apply, customize, and set default values for Layer Styles.

TOPIC A
Create Layers

You created images and modified the selections within them. However, there are limitations to working with one layer of pixels. Changes or errors made in one layer could result in much rework. In this topic, you will create layers.

You may have multiple objects or images as part of your design, and may need to alter just a specific one. Using layers, you can select and manipulate portions of your design you need to change, ensuring that the base layer remains unaffected and that the rework is avoided. You can also easily organize the objects or images in multiple layers, and group them to suit your needs.

Layers

Definition:

Layers are transparent pieces of an image that are stacked on top of one another to create a single image. When working with individual layers, you can rename, rearrange, or delete them without affecting other layers. When working with several layers, you can also selectively display or hide them to focus on specific areas of the image.

Example:

Figure 5-1: Objects distributed in individual layers.

Types of Layers

In Photoshop, there are different types of layers each having its own characteristics.

Layer Type	Description
Background	A layer that gets created automatically whenever a document is created or when an image is opened in Photoshop. There can be only one background layer in a Photoshop document. Because this layer holds the original data, it is advised not to perform any edit operation on this layer.
Image	A layer that contains image data.
Type or Text	A layer that contains text. This layer is used to edit and format text.
Shape	A type of layer created when you draw shapes using the Shape tools.
Fill	A layer that is filled with a solid color, gradient, or pattern. This layer is mostly used for creating special effects.
Adjustment	A layer that can be used to apply tonal or color changes to an image. The color and tonal adjustments are stored in this layer and get applied to all layers below it. Hence, multiple layers can be corrected with a single adjustment.
3D	A layer that contains 3D objects. Using a 2D layer, you can create 3D objects in Photoshop.
Smart Objects	A layer containing image information of either a raster or a vector image. This layer retains the original characteristics of the object and its source. It allows you to perform non-destructive editing to the object.

Nested Layer Groups

Two or more layers in a Photoshop document can be grouped as a layer group. Different layer groups can be nested together. This enables you to move and make changes to more than one layer group at a time. Nesting is an efficient way to keep different layer groups organized.

The LAYERS Panel

The **LAYERS** panel lists all layers, layer groups, and layer effects in an image. It displays each layer with a thumbnail view of the layer components along with its name. The visibility column can be used to hide or show layers. The eye icon next to the layer thumbnail in the **LAYERS** panel indicates layer visibility. You can use the lock controls available in the **LAYERS** panel to lock transparent portions of a layer, lock image pixels, lock only the layer position, or lock layer contents. The **LAYERS** panel has options that allow you to set the layer opacity and fill opacity, and apply various blending modes.

At the bottom of the **LAYERS** panel are listed various buttons that allow you to perform layer functions such as deleting a layer, creating a layer, creating a group, creating a fill or adjustment layer, adding a layer mask, adding layer styles, and linking layers. Additionally, you can also duplicate and group layers.

 A layer that is in selection in the panel and that is currently in use is said to be an active layer. All other layers are inactive layers.

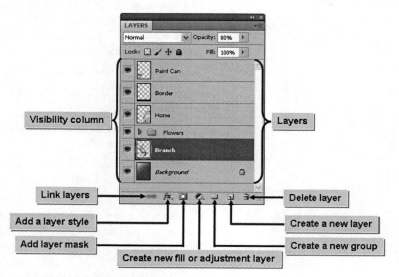

Figure 5-2: Components of the LAYERS panel.

Moving and Editing Layers

You can move layers or their contents using the **Move** tool. If you feel that editing a particular layer is essential, you can select it and perform the required editing actions.

How to Create Layers

Procedure Reference: Create a Layer

To create a layer:

1. If necessary, choose **Window→Layers** to display the **LAYERS** panel.
2. Create a layer.
    *   In the **LAYERS** panel, click the **Create a new layer** button or;
    *   At the top-right corner of the **LAYERS** panel, from the **LAYERS** panel options menu, choose **New Layer** and in the **New Layer** dialog box, specify the desired name and then click **OK** or;
    *   Choose **Layer→New→Layer.** In the **New Layer** dialog box, in the **Name** text box, type the desired name and then click **OK.**

 When you drag and drop an image file from any location into a document in the Photoshop application, it creates a layer.

3. If necessary, in the **LAYERS** panel, click in the layer visibility column to turn the visibility of the layer on or off.

4. If necessary, in the **LAYERS** panel, lock a selected layer.
    *   Click the **Lock transparent pixels** button to prevent changes in the transparent areas of the layer.
    *   Click the **Lock image pixels** button to prevent modifying the pixels of the layer.
    *   Click **Lock position** button to prevent moving the pixels of the layer.
    *   Click the **Lock all** button to lock all the options of the layer.

Procedure Reference: Duplicate a Layer

To duplicate a layer:

1. In the **LAYERS** panel, select a layer.
2. Display the **Duplicate Layer** dialog box.
    *   Choose **Layer→Duplicate Layer** or;
    *   From the **LAYERS** panel options menu, choose **Layer→Duplicate Layer** or;
    *   In the **LAYERS** panel, right-click a layer and choose **Duplicate Layer.**
3. In the **Duplicate Layer** dialog box, specify the desired settings.
    *   In the **As** text box, type a name for the duplicated layer.
    *   Specify the destination of the duplicated layer.
        *   In the **Destination** section, from the **Document** drop-down list, select the name of the document in which you want the duplicated layer to be placed.
        *   From the **Document** drop-down list, select **New** to place the duplicated layer in a new document.
        *   In the **Name** text box, type a name for the document.
4. Click **OK.**

 You can also drag a layer onto the **Create a new layer** button to duplicate a layer.

Procedure Reference: Create a Layer by Moving Selections to a New Layer

To create a layer by moving selections to a new layer:

1. Make a selection.
2. Move the selection to a new layer.
    *   Choose **Layer→New→Layer Via Cut** to cut the selected area and paste it in a new layer.
    *   Choose **Layer→New→Layer Via Copy** to copy the selected area and paste it in a new layer.

Procedure Reference: Rename a Layer

To rename a layer:

1. Select the layer to be renamed.
2. Right-click the layer or from the **LAYERS** panel options menu, choose **Layer Properties.**

3. In the **Layer Properties** dialog box, in the **Name** text box, type a name and click **OK.**

 You can also rename a layer by double-clicking the layer name, typing the desired name, and pressing **Enter.**

Procedure Reference: Move an Image in a Layer

To move an image in a layer:
1. In the **LAYERS** panel, select the layer to be moved.
2. Select the **Move** tool.
3. Click and drag the selected portion of the image to the desired location.

Procedure Reference: Merge Layers

To merge layers:
1. In the **LAYERS** panel, select two or more layers.
2. Choose **Layer→Merge Layers.**

 You can choose the **Merge Visible** command on the **Layer** menu to merge only the visible layers.

Procedure Reference: Delete a Layer

To delete a layer:
1. In the **LAYERS** panel, select the layer to be deleted.
2. Delete a layer.
   - In the **LAYERS** panel, click the **Delete layer** button. In the **Adobe Photoshop CS5 Extended** message box, click **Yes.**
   - Choose **Layer→Delete→Layer.** In the **Adobe Photoshop CS5 Extended** message box, click **Yes.**
   - Drag the layer to the **Delete layer** button.

 You can choose **Layer→Delete→Hidden Layers** to delete hidden layers.

ACTIVITY 5-1
Creating Layers

Data Files:

Color Sample Card.psd, Logo.png

Before You Begin:

1. Navigate to the C:\084384Data\Working with Layers folder and open the Color Sample Card.psd and Logo.png files.

2. Set the zoom percentage of the Color Sample Card document to 18.

Scenario:

While working on the color sample card, you want to include the logo of the company and add a background to the outer page of the color sample card. You moved images from different documents and placed each image on a different layer. You want to rename those layers appropriately so that you can easily identify them.

---

1. Import the logo onto the template.

   a. Display the Logo.png file in a floating window.

   b. In the **Tools** panel, select the **Move** tool.

   c. Click and drag the logo onto the Color Sample Card document.

   d. Close the Logo.png file.

---

2. Create the background for the color sample card and apply a color to it.

   a. Select the **LAYERS** panel and click the **Create a new layer** button.

   b. In the **Tools** panel, select the **Rectangular Marquee** tool. [ ]

   c. Scroll to the left and click and drag from the point of intersection of the 0-pixel mark on the horizontal and vertical rulers to the point of intersection of the 1400-pixel mark on the horizontal ruler and the 2800-pixel mark on the vertical ruler.

   > You are selecting the empty area on the left portion of the image in order to fill it with color.

   d. In the **Tools** panel, select the **Eyedropper** tool.

e.   Click below the lamp area to select the brick red color.

f.   From the **Gradient** tool flyout, select the **Paint Bucket** tool.

g.   Click in the selection to add the color fill.

h.   Deselect the selection.

3.   Rename the layers and delete the empty layer.

a.   In the **LAYERS** panel, double-click **Layer 6,** type *Background* and then press **Enter.**

b.   Double-click **Layer 4,** type *Green Paint Can* and then press **Enter.**

c.   Similarly, rename **Layer 3** as *Blue Paint Can* and **Layer 5** as *Logo* and then **Layer 2** as *Home*

d.   Select **Layer 1** and click the **Delete layer** button.

e.   In the **Adobe Photoshop CS5 Extended** message box, click **Yes.**

f.   Choose **File→Save As.**

g.   In the **Save As** dialog box, in the **File name** text box, type *My Color Sample Card* and click **Save.**

TOPIC B
Work with Type Layers

You created layers in a document. You may want to add content to the design you are creating and also customize it to increase its visual appeal and clarity. In this topic, you will enter text and alter the properties of text.

While looking through advertisements and brochures, how many times have you been impressed with an illustration that has a catchy slogan and is visually appealing? An effective image combined with well-written text lends context to the image, conveys the message more clearly, and attracts the reader's attention.

Type Layers

The *Type layer* is a layer that automatically gets added to the **LAYERS** panel when you use the **Type** tool for adding text in a document. Type layers have editable text that can be modified and formatted. Because they do not contain pixels, text can be resized dynamically without affecting its clarity.

Type Tools

There are two pairs of type tools in Photoshop—the horizontal and vertical type tools and the horizontal and vertical type mask tools. The **Horizontal Type** and **Vertical Type** tools are used to type text horizontally and vertically. The **Horizontal Type Mask** and **Vertical Type Mask** tools create a selection on the active layer in the shape of the text that is typed. The type mask tools are generally used to create masks in the shape of text.

Text Color and Placement

Choosing the appropriate color and placement of text will make text stand out. Placement of text should be based mainly on the type of text; the heading and caption, and other crucial information should be placed predominantly. Paragraphs, lengthy sentences, and additional information can be placed at the sides of images. Text color depends on the type and proportions of the text and background. The background and text color should be in contrast to each other. For example, for an image with light colors, choose text with dark colors and vice versa. Text that is not crucial to the message, such as author name, footer, or date, can have gray shades.

Text Properties

Because various factors can affect the readability of text, designers have to strike a balance between esthetic appeal and readability when selecting the font, size, type, and color of the text. The general guidelines for text properties are as follows:

- **Font Type:** There are many varieties of font types. Commonly used fonts are serif fonts such as Georgia and Times New Roman and sans-serif fonts such as Arial and Verdana. Use sans serif fonts for headings and serif fonts for paragraph text to ensure better readability. In addition, there are many stylish font types available and they can be used in appropriate situations.

- **Font Size:** Like font type, font size should help in easy readability. A font that is too small or too big will not appeal to readers. Using the right size for text throughout the document can help maintain consistency. For elements such as titles and subheadings and highlighted and lead-in text, size can vary.

- **Font Color:** The color of the font depends on that of the background. Use dark-colored text on light-colored backgrounds for better readability.

There are a few additional tips that developers can use to increase the readability and visual appearance of text.

- Use reasonable chunks of content.
- Use limited number of fonts.
- Use bold, italics, and capitalization wisely.
- Avoid using ALL CAPITALS in body text.
- Avoid lengthy sentences.

The Type Tool Options Bar

The **Type Tool** Options bar contains options that allow you to modify text in a document. You can use the options to change text orientation and select the font, font style, and font size. You can align text, choose a color for the text, and also apply warp to the text. Additional options allow you to toggle the display of the **CHARACTER** and **PARAGRAPH** panels.

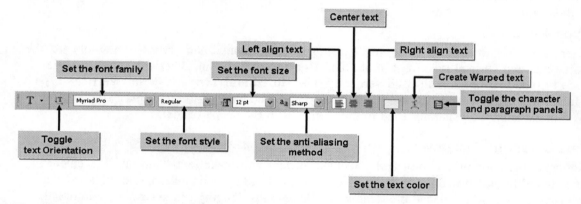

Figure 5-3: The Type Tool Options bar with its various options.

Using Anti-Aliasing Options

You can use anti-aliasing options to create smooth edges by partly filling pixels around the edge, so that the edges blend with the background.

The CHARACTER Panel

The **CHARACTER** panel contains options that allow you to select the font type, size, style, and color, and to set orientation of the typed text. You can increase the size of the text horizontally and vertically, and adjust the space between each text character by using the kerning options. Additionally, there are commands on the **CHARACTER** panel options menu that allow you to format text characters.

Figure 5-4: The CHARACTER panel used for formatting text characters.

Kerning

Kerning is the process of adjusting the spacing between text characters. For horizontal text, kerning applies to the horizontal distance between characters; and for vertical text, kerning applies to the vertical distance between characters.

The PARAGRAPH Panel

The **PARAGRAPH** panel contains options that allow you to format single or multiple paragraphs that are selected. You can indent, align, and justify the paragraph, and specify values to add space between each line in a paragraph and between paragraphs.

How to Work with Type Layers

Procedure Reference: Add Text to a Document

To add text to a document:

1. In the **LAYERS** panel, select the topmost layer.
2. Select the desired type tool.
3. In the document window, position the mouse pointer in the desired location and drag it to create a bounding box.
4. In the bounding box, type the desired text.
5. On the Options bar, click the **Commit any current edits** button to commit changes made to the type layer.
6. If necessary, click the **Cancel any current edits** button to cancel the changes made to the type layer.

Procedure Reference: Edit Type Properties

To edit type properties:

1. In the **LAYERS** panel, double-click the layer thumbnail of a type layer.
2. On the Options bar, specify the format settings.
   - From the **Set the font family** drop-down list, select the desired font.
   - From the **Set the font style** drop-down list, select the desired style.
   - In the **Set the font size** text box, specify the desired size.
     - Double-click and type the desired value or;
     - From the **Set the font size** drop-down list, select the desired value or;

- ■ Position the mouse pointer over the **Set the font size** icon and drag to specify the font size.

- ● From the **Set the anti-aliasing method** drop-down list, select the desired anti-aliasing method to be used.

- ● In the **Align** section, select the desired alignment style.

- ● Click the **Set the text color** box, and in the **Select text color** dialog box, select the desired color and click **OK.**

3. Click the **Commit any current edits** button.

4. If necessary, click the **Cancel any current edits** button to cancel the changes.

Procedure Reference: Format Text Using the CHARACTER Panel

To format text using the **CHARACTER** panel:

1. Select the text you want to format.

- ● Select the text with the **Selection** tool to format the entire text block or;
- ● Select the text with the **Type** tool to format certain words.

2. Display the **CHARACTER** panel.

- ● Choose **Window→Character** or;
- ● On the **Type** tool Options bar, click the **Toggle display of Character and Paragraph Panels** link.

3. In the **CHARACTER** panel, specify the formatting settings for the text.

- ● From the **Set the font family, Set the font style,** and **Set the font size** drop-down lists, select a font type, font style, and font size, respectively.

- ● From the **Set the leading** drop-down list, specify the spacing between the lines of text.

- ● From the **Set the kerning between two characters** drop-down list, select a value to adjust the spacing between two characters.

- ● From the **Set the tracking for the selected characters** drop-down list, select a value to loosen or tighten the spacing between characters.

- ● From the **Horizontally Scale** and **Vertically Scale** drop-down lists, set the width and height values.

- ● From the **Set the baseline shift** drop-down list, select a value to move characters up and down in line with the surrounding text.

- ● Click the **Set the text color** color box and in the **Select text color** dialog box, select a color.

- ● Click the **Underline** or **Strikethrough** button to apply an underline or strikethrough effect to the text.

- ● If necessary, click the **Faux Bold, Faux Italic, All Caps, Small Caps Superscript,** and **Subscript** buttons to format the text.

- ● From the **Set the language on selected characters for hyphenation and spelling** drop-down list, select a language.

- ● From the **Set the anti-aliasing method** drop-down list, select an anti-aliasing method.

Procedure Reference: Format a Paragraph Using the PARAGRAPH Panel

To format a paragraph using the **PARAGRAPH** panel:

1. Select the text you want to format.
   - Select the text with the **Selection** tool to format the entire text block or;
   - Select the text with the **Type** tool to format certain words.
2. Display the **PARAGRAPH** panel.
   - Choose **Window→Paragraph** or;
   - On the **Type** tool Options bar, click the **Toggle display of Character and Paragraph Panels** link.
3. In the **PARAGRAPH** panel, specify the formatting settings.
   - Click **Left align text** to left align the text or a paragraph.
   - Click **Center text** to center align the text or a paragraph.
   - Click **Right align text** to right align the text or a paragraph.

 If necessary, click the other buttons to justify the paragraph.

   - In the **Indent left margin** and **Indent right margin** text boxes, specify a value to indent a paragraph.
   - In the **Indent first line** text box, specify a value to indent the first line of each paragraph.
   - Specify a value in the **Add space before paragraph** text box or in the **Add space after paragraph** text box, to provide spacing between paragraphs.
   - Check the **Automatic hyphenation** check box to hyphenate specific words in the paragraph.

ACTIVITY 5-2
Working with Type Layers

Data Files:

My Color Sample Card.psd

Before You Begin:

The My Color Sample Card.psd file is open.

Scenario:

After creating product layers, you may want to enhance the appearance of the document to make it look presentable and professional. For this purpose, you may want to add content to the color sample card, change the default font, and enhance its appearance.

---

1. Set text formatting and enter text for the paint cans.

    a. In the **Tools** panel, select the **Horizontal Type** tool.

    b. On the Options bar, from the **Set the font family** drop-down list, scroll up and select **Arial.**

    c. In the **Set the font size** text box, click and drag over the value, type **20** and then press **Enter.**

    d. Click the **Set the text color** box.

    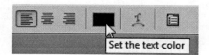

    e. In the **Select text color** dialog box, in the # text box, double-click, type **ffd790** and then click **OK.**

    f. In the **LAYERS** panel, click and drag the Background layer and then place it below the Blue Paint Can layer when a black line appears.

    g. Below and to the left of the blue paint can, click and type **Hexa Standard**

    h. On the Options bar, click the **Commit any current edits** button.

    i. With the **Horizontal Type** tool selected, click to the right of the existing text, and under the green paint can, type **Hexa Supreme**

    j. On the Options bar, click the **Commit any current edits** button to set the text on the layer.

---

2. Modify text format and enter the marketing byline for the color sample card.

    a. Click at the point of intersection of the 1950-pixel mark on the horizontal ruler and the 200-pixel mark on the vertical ruler.

    b. From the **Set the font family** drop-down list, scroll down and select **Edo.**

c. In the **Set the font size** text box, double-click the value and type *47*

d. Display the **Select text color** dialog box and in the # text box, double-click, type *FFFFFF* and then click **OK.**

e. Type *PAINT YOUR DREAMS!!!*

f. Click after the letter "R" in the word "YOUR" and press **Enter** to split the phrase into two lines.

g. On the Options bar, click the **Commit any current edits** button.

h. Save the file.

TOPIC C
Transform Layers

You worked with type layers. At times, you may be required to resize, rotate, or reshape layers or selected areas in a layer. In this topic, you will transform layers.

While working on a selected layer, you might feel the need to resize or reposition the layer. Transforming the layers in an image helps you modify them according to your needs.

The Free Transform Command

A layer or a selection can be transformed using the **Free Transform** command. A bounding box with transform handles is displayed around the selection when this command is chosen. The transform handles in the middle of each side of the box are used to drag and resize the image's height or width. The transform handles at the corners of the box are used to resize the height and width of the image proportionately.

The Free Transform Command Options

The **Free Transform** command Options bar allows you to apply more transform effects to a selection.

Option	Allows You To
Reference point location	Change the reference point of the selection.
Set horizontal position of reference point	Set the X position of the object relative to its reference point.
Set vertical position of reference point	Set the Y position of the object relative to its reference point.
Set horizontal scale	Set the value in percentage to increase or decrease the scaling of the object horizontally.
Maintain aspect ratio	Maintain the same aspect ratio between the horizontal and vertical scale percentage.
Set vertical scale	Set the value in percentage to increase or decrease the scaling of the object vertically.
Set rotation	Specify the degree to rotate a selection.
Set horizontal skew	Specify the degree for skewing a selection horizontally.
Set vertical skew	Specify the degree for skewing a selection vertically.

The Transform Menu Commands

The **Transform** menu commands allow you to apply a transform effect to an image.

Command	*Allows You To*
Scale	Increase or decrease an object relative to its reference point or the point of transformation of an object.
Rotate	Rotate an object around its reference point to the required degree.
Skew	Slant an object vertically or horizontally.
Distort	Stretch an object in all directions.
Perspective	Skew an image that is on a flat surface to create a farther or closer realistic representation of it as seen by the naked eye.
Warp	Adjust the gridlines in the bounding box to change the appearance of an object.
Rotate 180°, Rotate 90° CW, and **Rotate 90° CCW**	Rotate the object to the specified degree in the clockwise or counterclockwise direction as the command name reads.
Flip Horizontal and **Flip Vertical**	Turn the object horizontally or vertically.

Transform Defaults

Transformations are based on the selected reference point. By default, Photoshop transforms areas based on the center point of the selected area.

Canvas Rotation

The transform commands allow you to rotate or flip one or more selected layers. You can use the commands available on the **Image Rotation** submenu of the **Image** menu to rotate or flip the entire canvas. Transforming the canvas will transform all the layers in a document.

How to Transform Layers

Procedure Reference: Select Layers

To select layers:

1. Choose **Window→Layers** to display the **LAYERS** panel.
2. Select layers.
   - Select layers using the **LAYERS** panel.
     - In the **LAYERS** panel, select a layer or;
     - Select a layer, hold down **Shift,** and select the layers below or above to select multiple layers.
   - Select the layers using menu commands.
     - Choose **Select→All Layers** to select all the layers or;
     - Choose **Select→Similar Layers** to select layers that are similar.
   - Select layers in the document window using the **Move** tool.
     - On the Options bar, check the **Auto-Select** check box, and from the **Auto-Select** drop-down list, select **Layer** and then select the layer in the document or;
     - Right-click the image and choose a layer.
3. If necessary, deselect layers.
   - Press **Ctrl** and select the layer to deselect it.
   - Choose **Select→Deselect Layers** to deselect all the layers.

Procedure Reference: Transform a Selection Using the Free Transform Command

To transform a selection using the **Free Transform** command:

1. In the **LAYERS** panel, select the desired layer.
2. If necessary, make a selection in the selected layer.
3. Choose **Edit→Free Transform.**
4. Transform the selection.
   - Click and drag the transform handle to scale the selection.

 Hold down **Shift** as you drag the transform handle to scale the selection proportionately.

 Hold down **Ctrl** as you drag the transform handles to skew an image.

- Position the mouse pointer outside the transform handles, and click and drag the double-headed arrow to rotate the selection.
- Hold down **Ctrl** and click and drag the corner handles diagonally up or down to warp the selection.
- Hold down **Ctrl** and click and drag the top-middle or bottom-middle transform handles to shear the selection.
- Click and drag the transform handle to the opposite side of the bounding box to flip the image.

5. Apply the transformation.
   - Press **Enter** or;
   - On the Options bar, click the **Commit transform (Return)** button or;
   - Double-click in the transformation marquee.
6. If necessary, cancel the transformation.
   - Press **Esc** or;
   - On the Options bar, click the **Cancel transform** button.

Procedure Reference: Transform a Selection Using the Transform Command

To transform a selection using the **Transform** command:
1. Select the desired layer.
2. If necessary, make a selection in the selected layer.
3. Choose **Edit→Transform** and then choose the appropriate command to transform.
   - Choose **Scale** and perform the desired action to scale the selection.

 The reference point can be selected by clicking a square in the **Reference point location**. The horizontal position of the reference point can be set by using the **Set horizontal position of reference point** text box and the vertical position of the reference point by using the **Set vertical position of reference point** text box.

   - Click and drag the transform handle or;
   - On the Options bar, in the **Set horizontal scale** and **Set vertical scale** text boxes, specify values for the horizontal and vertical scales or place the mouse pointer over **W** and **H** and then drag to specify the width and height in percentage.
   - Choose **Rotate** and perform the desired action to rotate the selection.
      - Position the mouse pointer outside the bounding box and drag the curved, double-headed arrow or;
      - On the Options bar, in the **Rotate** text box, specify the degrees or place the mouse pointer over the **Rotate** icon and then drag to specify the degrees.

 Hold down **Shift** as you drag the transform handle of the selection to rotate it in 15° increments.

   - Choose **Skew** and perform the desired action to slant an item.

- Click and drag a side handle or;
- On the Options bar, set the horizontal and vertical skew or place the mouse pointer over the **Set horizontal skew** icon or the **Set vertical skew** icon and then drag to specify the values for the skew.

- Choose **Flip Horizontal** or **Flip Vertical** to flip the selection horizontally along the vertical axis or vertically along the horizontal axis.

4. Apply the transformation.
5. If necessary, cancel the transformation.

Procedure Reference: Rotate a Canvas Using the Image Menu

To rotate a canvas using the **Image** menu:

1. Open a Photoshop document.
2. Rotate the canvas.

- Choose **Image→Image Rotation→180°** to rotate the canvas at 180 degrees.
- Choose **Image→Image Rotation→90° CW** to rotate the canvas at 90 degrees in the clockwise direction.
- Choose **Image→Image Rotation→90° CCW** to rotate the canvas at 90 degrees in the counter clockwise direction.
- Choose **Image→Image Rotation→Arbitrary** to specify an angle and direction by which the canvas will be rotated.

 The **Rotate View** tool in the **Tools** panel allows you to rotate an image without transforming it. This gives the feeling of rotating an image drawn on paper and makes it easy to work on screen. This tool can be selected from the **Tools** panel or from the Application bar.

Procedure Reference: Flip a Canvas Using the Image Menu

To flip a canvas using the **Image** menu:

1. Open a Photoshop document.
2. Choose **Image→Image Rotation→Flip Canvas Horizontal** to flip the canvas horizontally.
3. Choose **Image→Image Rotation→Flip Canvas Vertical** to flip the canvas vertically.

Procedure Reference: Straighten Images

To crop and straighten an image:

1. In the **Tools** panel, select the **Ruler** tool.
2. Click and drag to the desired point over the image.
3. On the Options bar, click the **Straighten** button to rotate, scale, or crop the image.

 You may also use the **File→Automate→Crop and Straighten Photos** command to crop and straighten an image.

ACTIVITY 5-3
Transforming Layers

Data Files:

My Color Sample Card.psd, Main Paint Can.png

Before You Begin:

The My Color Sample Card.psd file is open.

Scenario:

You need to add and position the paint can image to the cover page of the color sample card. The size of the image is big. Additionally, you are required to position the elements that are already available in the color sample card so that they look appealing.

---

1. Place the paint cans and the logo appropriately.

    a. In the **Tools** panel, select the **Move** tool.

    b. Select the Green Paint Can layer and choose **Edit→Free Transform.**

    c. On the Options bar, in the **X** text box, click and drag over the value, type *1007.5* and then press **Tab.**

    d. In the **Y** text box, type *2272* and then click the **Commit transform (Return)** button.

    e. Select the "Hexa Supreme" text and position it below the green paint can image.

    f. Select the Logo layer and choose **Edit→Free Transform.**

    g. On the Options bar, specify the values for **X** and **Y** as *701.5* and *1051.5* respectively.

    h. Click the **Commit transform (Return)** button.

---

2. Import the paint can image for the cover page.

    a. Select the Home layer.

    b. Open the Main Paint Can.png file from the C:\084384Data\Working with Layers folder.

    c. Display the file as a floating window.

    d. Click and drag the can to place it in the bottom-right corner of the home image.

    e. Close the Main Paint Can.png file.

     f.   In the **LAYERS** panel, rename the new layer as ***Main Paint Can***

3.   Transform the paint can image to fit into the cover page.

     a.   Choose **Edit→Transform→Scale.**

     b.   On the Options bar, in the **W** text box, double-click, type *82.9* and then press **Tab.**

     c.   In the **H** text box, type *82.9* and press **Enter.**

     d.   On the Options bar, specify the values for **X** and **Y** as *2360* and *2303* respectively.

     e.   Click the **Commit transform (Return)** button.

4.   Remove the number from the home image on the cover page.

     a.   In the **LAYERS** panel, select the Home layer.

     b.   In the **Tools** panel, select the **Rectangular Marquee** tool.

     c.   Click and drag from the point of intersection of the 1750-pixel mark on the horizontal ruler and the 1700-pixel mark on the vertical ruler to the point of intersection of the 1900-pixel mark on the horizontal ruler and the 1800-pixel mark on the vertical ruler.

     d.   Choose **Edit→Free Transform.**

     e.   Drag the bottom-middle handle downward to hide the house number.

     f.   Click the **Commit transform (Return)** button.

     g.   Deselect the selection.

     h.   Save the file.

TOPIC D
Apply Styles

You transformed objects. You may now want to enhance the objects to achieve the desired effect. In this topic, you will apply layer styles.

A dull looking brochure in spite of having good content is sure to bore its readers compared to a color packed and content relevant brochure. This goes on to show that enhancing the visual appeal of a design has greater impact. Rather than a plain graphic or text, a customized and colorful design is bound to grab the attention of the viewer.

Opacity

Opacity refers to the degree of transparency in a layer. The lower you set the layer opacity, the more transparent the layer appears. When you adjust a layer's opacity, the transparency effect is applied equally to the entire layer. However, in order to achieve realistic effects, some areas within the layer may need higher or lower opacity.

Blending Modes

Blending modes can be used to create a variety of effects by blending pixels in a layer or between layers. Photoshop contains a number of blending modes. The blending modes control how pixels in the image will be affected. Some of the blending modes are **Difference, Multiply, Overlay, Hard Light,** and **Soft Light.** The **Difference** blending mode compares the brightness value of the current layer's color with that of the color of the lower layers, and applies the resultant colors. The **Multiply** blending mode allows you to maintain the transparency of the original layer while strengthening the solidity of the dark areas in an image, making the image appear more solid. The other blending modes, such as **Overlay, Hard Light,** and **Soft Light,** allow you to create semi-transparent effects.

Blending Mode Options

There are different blending mode options using which you can create effects by blending pixels in layers. Some of the blending modes are described in the table.

Blending Mode Option	Function
Normal	Displays the pixels of an image in exact colors. This is the default mode in Photoshop.
Dissolve	Blends the edge pixels to create an effect of scattered pixels along the edges.
Screen	Multiplies the inverse of the colors in the pixels of the blended and base colors.
Color Dodge	Decreases the color contrast between two colors.
Darken	Displays the darker of the pixels from the blended layers.
Multiply	Multiplies the pixels in the blended layers resulting in a darker image.

Blending Mode Option	Function
Overlay	Overlays the pixels in the base layer while retaining the shadow and highlight details.
Soft Light	Darkens or lightens color, creating an effect of diffused light illuminating the image.
Hard Light	Produces an effect of a spotlight illuminating the image.
Luminosity	Retains the hue and saturation of the base image and the luminance of the blended image.

Blending Modes for Various Tools

For each tool that you choose, the blending mode options that are displayed on the Options bar vary. Blending mode options are available for most of the tools such as **Brush, Healing, Clone Stamp, History, Paint Bucket, Eraser,** and so on. For example, if you select the **Paint Bucket** tool, blending mode options such as **Darken, Multiply, Lighten, Color Dodge, Overlay, Soft Light, Hard Light, Difference, Exclusion,** and many more will be available.

Apply Blending Modes to a Group

You can apply blending modes to a layer group. By default, the blending mode of a group is **Pass Through;** the group has no blending properties. When you select a blending mode for a group, the group is treated as a single unit and is blended with the rest of the image using the selected blending mode. The blending mode for a group will override any blending modes applied to an individual layer belonging to the group.

Layer Styles

Layer styles are special effects that can be applied to individual layers. Photoshop has predefined layer styles that can be applied to layers. These styles are listed in the **Layer Style** dialog box. You can preview the style before applying it and also define new styles. The options displayed in the **Layer Style** dialog box will vary according to the style that you select. Layer styles are automatically applied to any new content added to the layer. Because the style is a separate entity and is just linked to the layer, it updates itself as and when layer contents are modified or moved.

The STYLES Panel

The **STYLES** panel in Photoshop contains varied preset styles that can be applied to layers. You can also create customized styles using the panel. The panel contains a number of components that can be used to clear, create, and delete styles.

How to Apply Styles

Procedure Reference: Set the Opacity for a Layer

To set the opacity for a layer:

1. Select the layer to set its opacity.

2. In the **LAYERS** panel, specify the opacity level for the layer.

    *   Click the triangle to the right of the **Opacity** text box, and drag the opacity slider to the desired opacity level or;

    *   In the **Opacity** text box, specify the desired opacity value.

Procedure Reference: Apply a Layer Style

To apply a layer style:

1. In the **LAYERS** panel, select a layer.

    *   Select a layer that contains images to apply layer styles to images.

    *   Select a type layer to apply layer styles to text.

2. Apply the desired layer style.

    *   Choose **Layer→Layer Style** and then choose the desired layer style.

    *   In the **LAYERS** panel, from the **Add a layer style** drop-down list, select the desired layer style.

    *   Select the desired layer style in the **Layer Style** dialog box.

        a. Choose **Layer→Layer Style→Blending Options** or in the **LAYERS** panel, from the **Add a layer style** drop-down list, select **Blending Options** to display the **Layer Style** dialog box.

        b. In the **Layer Style** dialog box, in the left pane, select the desired style and in the right pane, specify the settings.

        c. Click **OK.**

    *   In the **STYLES** panel, select the desired layer style.

3. If necessary, remove the applied layer styles.

    *   In the **STYLES** panel, select the style and click the **Clear Style** or **Delete Style** button or;

    *   Choose **Layer→Layer Style→Clear Layer Style** or;

    *   In the selected layer, drag the **Indicates layer effects** icon to the **Delete** button at the bottom of the **LAYERS** panel to remove all the styles applied or;

    *   Drag the **Effects** layer style to the **Delete** button at the bottom of the **LAYERS** panel to remove all the styles applied or;

    *   In the selected layer, drag a layer style to the **Delete** button at the bottom of the **LAYERS** panel to remove the selected effect.

ACTIVITY 5-4
Applying Layer Styles

Data Files:

My Color Sample Card.psd

Before You Begin:

The My Color Sample Card.psd file is open.

Scenario:

A coworker suggests that by applying effects you can improve the visual appeal of your design. You agree and also realize that the cover design of the color sample card appears cluttered, detracting attention from the product. With some modifications, you can add more focus on the product. You also decide to add an effect to the marketing text. Because you are trying out different options, and know that not all of the effects you try out will meet your expectations, you remind yourself that you can remove those that do not create the desired outcome.

---

1. Apply a glow effect and specify the desired settings.

    a. In the **LAYERS** panel, select the Main Paint Can layer.

    b. Choose **Layer→Layer Style→Outer Glow.**

    c. In the **Layer Style** dialog box, in the **Structure** section, from the **Blend Mode** drop-down list, select **Normal.**

    d. In the **Opacity** text box, double-click and type *92*

    e. Click the **Set color of glow** box.

    f. In the **Color Picker** dialog box, in the **#** text box, double-click, type *ffffff* and then click **OK.**

    g. In the **Elements** section, in the **Spread** text box, double-click and type *46*

    h. In the **Size** text box, double-click and type *103*

    i. In the **Quality** section, in the **Range** text box, double-click and type *92*

    j. In the **Quality** section, in the **Jitter** text box, double-click, type *68* and then click **OK.**

---

2. Apply an effect to the title.

    a. In the **LAYERS** panel, select the PAINT YOUR DREAMS!!! layer.

    b. Click the **Add a layer style** button and select **Drop Shadow** to display the **Layer Style** dialog box.

c.   In the **Opacity** text box, type *31*

d.   In the **Distance** text box, double-click and type *30*

e.   In the **Spread** text box, double-click and type *9*

f.   In the **Size** text box, double-click, type *27* and then click **OK.**

3.   Apply more effects to the title to enhance its appearance.

a.   Click the **Add a layer style** button and select **Bevel and Emboss.**

b.   In the **Layer Style** dialog box, in the **Structure** section, in the **Size** text box, double-click and type *62*

c.   In the **Soften** text box, double-click, type *4* and then click **OK.**

d.   Click the **Add a layer style** button and select **Outer Glow.**

e.   In the **Elements** section, from the **Technique** drop-down list, select **Precise** and then click **OK.**

 Do not save the file now.

TOPIC E
Undo Previous Steps

You applied styles to layers. In the process, you may have thought of undoing or redoing a particular action or process itself. In this topic, you will undo previous steps.

When you have to perform multiple actions on different layers, you may find it difficult to keep track of changes in each layer. You may find the need to undo certain actions you have performed or redo certain actions. Photoshop provides you with options that allow you to undo and redo previous actions.

Tools to Undo Previous Actions

Photoshop offers several approaches that allow you to undo previous actions.

The following table describes some of the correction tools.

Tool	Used To
Eraser tool	Erase pixels in the active layer. However, when the default background layer is the active layer, this tool does not erase pixels but changes their color to the background color.
Undo command	Undo only the most recent command or action.
HISTORY panel	Undo multiple steps and return the entire image to its previous state.
History Brush tool	Return specific areas of an image to its previous state, without affecting the rest of the image. This is useful if you want to correct a mistake you made several steps before, without undoing the steps in between.

The HISTORY Panel

The *HISTORY panel* keeps track of all the menu choices, transforms, and effects that are applied to an image. You can use these steps to return the image to an earlier stage of development. The top state in the **HISTORY** panel contains the state of an image as it appeared the last time you saved it.

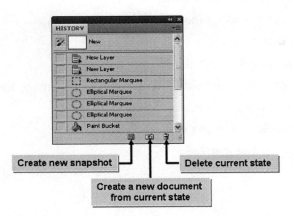

Figure 5-5: *Actions performed in a document are listed in the HISTORY panel.*

How to Undo Previous Steps

Procedure Reference: Undo Steps Using the HISTORY Panel

To undo steps using the **HISTORY** panel:

1. Choose **Window→History.**
2. In the **HISTORY** panel, select the state that needs to be reverted.
3. Undo steps.
   - Click the **Delete current state** button and in the **Adobe Photoshop CS5 Extended** message box, click **OK.**
   - Drag the **History** state slider upward to revert to the previous state.
4. If necessary, drag the **History** state slider downward to redo the steps.

Procedure Reference: Revert to the Previous Image State Using the History Brush Tool

To revert to the previous image state using the **History Brush** tool:

1. Select the desired layer.
2. Select the **History Brush** tool.
3. On the Options bar, click the drop-down arrow next to the **Brush** icon.
4. In the list, select a brush tip.
5. Click the drop-down arrow again to hide the list.
6. Click and drag the mouse pointer over the areas of the image that need to be reverted to the earlier state.
7. If necessary, choose **File→Revert** to return to the last saved state of the image.

Procedure Reference: Undo Previous Actions

To undo previous actions:

1. Select the image whose action needs to be undone.
2. Undo previous actions.
   - Undo previous actions using the menu commands.
     - Choose **Edit→Undo** *<previous action>* or;

- Choose **Edit→Step Backward.**
- Undo previous actions using the **Eraser** tool.
    a. Select the desired layer.
    b. In the **Tools** panel, select the **Eraser** tool.
    c. Click and drag over the particular portion of the image to erase it.

3. If necessary, redo an undone action.
   - Choose **Edit→Redo** *<previous action>* or;
   - Choose **Edit→Step Forward.**

ACTIVITY 5-5
Undoing Previous Steps

Data Files:
My Color Sample Card.psd

Before You Begin:
The My Color Sample Card.psd file is open.

Scenario:
You are not satisfied with the effects applied to the text. Also, the look and feel of the effect is not very appealing. So, you decide to remove some of the effects applied to the text.

1. Undo the previous steps.

    a. Choose **Edit→Undo Outer Glow** to remove the previously applied effect.

    b. Choose **Window→History.**

    c. In the **HISTORY** panel, verify that **Bevel and Emboss** is selected.

    d. At the bottom of the **HISTORY** panel, click the **Delete current state** button, 🗑 to delete the selected effect.

    e. In the **Adobe Photoshop CS5 Extended** message box, click **Yes.**

2. Close the **HISTORY** panel and save the file.

    a. Close the **HISTORY** panel using the panel options menu.

    b. Save the file.

TOPIC F
Manage Layers

You performed undo actions to restore the previous state of an image. To organize the document in order, you may have to perform certain tasks. In this topic, you will manage layers.

When you have multiple images in a document, you can easily select and edit the images individually when each exists on a separate layer. In case of an image with multiple layers, identifying a layer and working with it would be difficult if the layers are not organized. Photoshop provides you with options that allow you to group, arrange, align, and distribute layers.

Stacking Order of Layers

When working with multiple layers, you might have parts of an image overlapping other layers and affecting the display of the contents. You can prevent this by changing the stacking order of layers in the **LAYERS** panel. Layers that are at the top of the panel will appear in the front. You can change the stacking order by dragging the layer in the **LAYERS** panel.

Arranging Layers

The images in layers that are topmost in the stacking order will appear above the images in layers that are lowest in the stacking order.

Linking Layers

In Photoshop, you can link two or more layers or layer groups. By linking layers, you can move the images of the linked layers simultaneously, thereby saving time.

Layer Groups

Layer groups allow you to organize layers into batches that can be collapsed or expanded in the **LAYERS** panel. You can move, hide, or show all layers at once and rearrange them as a group.

The Alignment and Distribution Options

The alignment options allow you to align the contents of an image either horizontally or vertically within the document. You can use the horizontal alignment options to align the content to the top edges, vertical centers, or the bottom edges of the document. You can use the vertical alignment options to align the content to the left edges, horizontal centers, or the right edges of the document. Similar to the alignment options, the distribution options are used to position multiple objects in a document either at the top or bottom edges, vertical or horizontal centers.

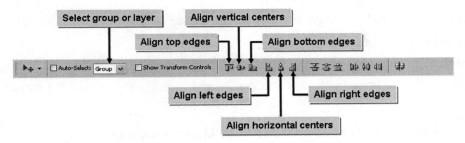

Figure 5-6: Alignment options on the Options bar that can be used to align objects.

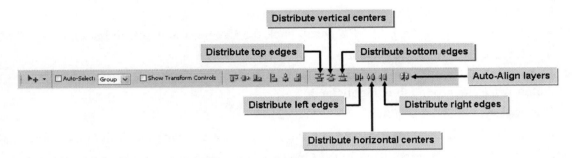

Figure 5-7: Distribution options on the Options bar that can be used to position objects evenly.

Advantages of Merging Layers

Merging is a feature that allows you to merge the content of the selected layers with that of the top layer. Merging is performed after finalizing the content of the layers and it helps in reducing the image size. You can use the merge commands on the **LAYERS** panel options menu to merge layers in an image. For merging layers, you will need to select the appropriate layer or group and then choose the merge command based on the requirements.

Image Flattening

Image flattening in Photoshop merges all visible layers into the background. All hidden layers are discarded and transparent areas are filled with white. By *flattening* images using the **Flatten Image** command, you can merge all layers to form a background layer. Like merging, flattening an image also reduces its file size.

File Size Reduction

The number of pixels in an image determines its file size. Combining layers or flattening the image reduces the number of pixels in the image just as pixels on lower layers are replaced by pixels that overlap them on higher layers.

Difference Between Layered Files and Flattened Files

In a Photoshop document, layered files refer to a document which has layers of an image organized one below the other sequentially. Flattened files refer to a document that contains only the flattened image.

How to Manage Layers

Procedure Reference: Change the Stacking Order of Layers

To change the stacking order of layers:

1. In the **LAYERS** panel, select the layer you want to move.
2. Drag the selected layer up or down to the desired location and release the mouse button to position the corresponding images accordingly.

Procedure Reference: Create a Group with Multiple Layers

To create a group with multiple layers:

1. Open a Photoshop document.
2. Create a group.
   - At the bottom of the **LAYERS** panel, click the **Create a new group** button or;
   - Choose **Layers→New→Group.**
3. In the **LAYERS** panel, drag the desired layers into the group and then release the mouse button when the group tab is highlighted.
4. If necessary, rename the group.
   - In the **LAYERS** panel, double-click the group name and type the desired name or;
   - Double-click the group, and in the **Group Properties** dialog box, in the **Name** text box, type the desired name and click **OK** or;
   - In the **LAYERS** panel, select **Group Properties,** and in the **Name** text box, type the desired name and click **OK** or;
   - Choose **Layer→Group Properties,** and in the **Name** text box, type the desired name and click **OK.**
5. If necessary, within a group, create a group to nest the layer group.

Procedure Reference: Move Images in a Group

To move images in a group:

1. In the **LAYERS** panel, select a group to move its images.
2. In the document window, drag one of the objects.

Procedure Reference: Set Layer Links

To link layers:

1. Select the layers to be linked.
   a. Select a layer.
   b. Hold down **Ctrl** and select the layers to be linked.
2. Link the selected layers.
   - At the bottom of the **LAYERS** panel, click the **Link layers** button or;
   - Choose **Layer→Link Layers.**

Procedure Reference: Remove Layer Links

To remove layer links:

1. Select one of the linked layers.

2. Remove the link for the selected layers.

    ●   At the bottom of the **LAYERS** panel, click the **Link layers** button or;

    ●   Choose **Layer→Select Linked Layers** and then choose **Layer→Unlink Layers.**

Procedure Reference: Delete a Group

To delete a group:

1. Select the group you want to delete.

2. Delete a group.

    ●   In the **LAYERS** panel, click the **Delete layer** button. In the **Adobe Photoshop CS5 Extended** message box, click **Yes** or;

    ●   Drag a group to the **Delete layer** button or;

    ●   With the **Move** tool active, press **Delete** or;

    ●   From the **LAYERS** panel options menu, choose **Delete Group** or;

    ●   Press **Alt** and click the **Delete layer** button.

Procedure Reference: Align and Distribute Multiple Layers

To align and distribute layers:

1. In the **LAYERS** panel, select the layers to be aligned and distributed.

 The align buttons are enabled when you select more than one layer, and the distribute buttons are enabled when you select more than two layers.

2. Align and distribute multiple layers.

    ●   On the Options bar, click the desired button to align the layers.

 Alignment and distribution options are displayed on the Options bar only when you select the **Move** tool or **Path Selection** tool.

    ■   Click the **Align top edges** button to align the images to the top edge for all the selected layers in the document.

    ■   Click the **Align vertical centers** button to align the images to the vertical center for all the selected layers in the document.

    ■   Click the **Align bottom edges** button to align the images to the bottom edge for all the selected layers in the document.

    ■   Click the **Align left edges** button to align the images to the left edge for all the selected layers in the document.

    ■   Click the **Align horizontal centers** button to align the images to the horizontal centers for all the selected layers in the document.

    ■   Click the **Align right edges** button to align the images to the right edge for all the selected layers in the document.

    ●   On the Options bar, click the desired buttons to distribute the layers.

    ■   Click the **Distribute top edges** button to space the layers evenly starting from the top edge of each layer.

- Click the **Distribute vertical centers** button to space the layers evenly starting from the vertical center of each layer.

- Click the **Distribute bottom edges** button to space the layers evenly starting from the bottom edge of each layer.

- Click the **Distribute left edges** button to space the layers evenly starting from the left edge of each layer.

- Click the **Distribute horizontal centers** button to space the layers evenly starting from the horizontal center of each layer.

- Click the **Distribute right edges** button to space the layers evenly starting from the right edge of each layer.

Procedure Reference: Merge Layers

To merge layers:

1. In the **LAYERS** panel, select the layers to be merged.
2. From the **LAYERS** panel options menu, choose the desired merging command.
   - Choose **Merge Group** to merge layers in a group.
   - Choose **Merge Layers** to merge selected layers.
   - Choose **Merge Down** to merge the selected layer with the layer below it.

Procedure Reference: Flatten Images

To flatten images:

1. In the **LAYERS** panel, select the layer to be flattened.
2. From the **LAYERS** panel options menu, choose **Flatten Image.**

ACTIVITY 5-6
Managing Layers

Data Files:

My Color Sample Card.psd

Before You Begin:

The My Color Sample Card.psd file is open.

Scenario:

You created multiple images, which are placed on different layers. The cluttered appearance of the number of layers makes it difficult to locate a particular layer on which you want to work. You also want a few of the layers to be grouped so that they can be moved or modified as one single component. Also, you want to adjust the position of the text and paint can image evenly.

---

1. Arrange layers and group the components of the right and left side of the cover design.

    a. Click and drag the PAINT YOUR DREAMS!!! layer and place it below the Background layer.

    b. Scroll down and verify that the PAINT YOUR DREAMS!!! layer is selected, hold down **Shift,** and select the Home layer.

    c. Choose **Layer→Group Layers.**

    d. Verify that the layers have been grouped to form **Group 1.**

    e. Select the Background layer, hold down **Shift,** and select the Logo layer.

    f. Choose **Layer→Group Layers** to group layers as **Group 2.**

---

2. Align the text and paint cans on the front cover page of the Color Sample Card.

    a. Expand Group 1 to view the layers in it.

    b. Select the PAINT YOUR DREAMS!!! layer.

    c. Hold down **Ctrl** and select the Main Paint Can layer.

    d. In the **Tools** panel, select the **Move** tool.

    e. On the Options bar, click the **Align right edges** button to align the text and the paint can to the right edge of the front cover page.

    f. Expand Group 2 to view the layers in it.

g. Select the Blue Paint Can layer along with the Hexa Standard layer.

h. On the Options bar, click the **Align horizontal centers** button to align the text and the paint can based on the horizontal centers.

i. Select the Green Paint Can layer along with the Hexa Supreme layer.

j. On the Options bar, click the **Align horizontal centers** button to align the text and the paint can based on the horizontal centers.

k. Select the Green Paint Can and Blue Paint Can layers.

l. On the Options bar, click the **Align bottom edges** button to align the cans to the bottom edges.

m. Select the Hexa Supreme and Hexa Standard layers. On the Options bar, click the **Align bottom edges** button to align the text layers to the bottom edges.

n. Save and close the file.

Lesson 5 Follow-up

In this lesson, you used layers to isolate specific parts of an image. You can easily avoid errors such as selecting and saving a wrong area if you work with individual parts of an image. Layers provide an easy and efficient way of organizing and editing composite images.

1. **How will you use the *LAYERS* panel to create composite images?**

2. **What are the effects that you often apply to layers? Why?**

6 Enhancing Images with Paint and Filters

Lesson Time: 30 minutes

Lesson Objectives:

In this lesson, you will enhance images with paint and filters.

You will:

● Paint on an image.

● Apply filter effects.

Introduction

You worked with layers and manipulated images in your document. Adobe® Photoshop® CS5 allows you to enhance the quality of images using various tools and methods. In this lesson, you will enhance images to improve their quality.

You may not initially be satisfied with your design and may want to modify it to get the best result. Using Photoshop's numerous options for applying special effects to an image, or an image layer, enables you to create a limitless variety of interesting effects. This will help enhance images. However, the more effects you use, the greater the size of your file. Photoshop allows you to merge and flatten images, thereby reducing the file size.

This lesson covers all or part of the following Adobe Visual Communication using Photoshop CS5 objectives:

● Topic A

  ■ Objective 4.4c: Identify advanced adjustment tools and when to use them.

  ■ Objective 4.4h: Demonstrate knowledge of opacity and fill.

  ■ Objective 4.6c: Identify tools that are used for painting.

  ■ Objective 4.6f: Demonstrate knowledge of color blending.

● Topic B

  ■ Objective 4.8a: Demonstrate knowledge of how to use the Filter Gallery.

  ■ Objective 4.8e: Identify the appropriate filter to use for a variety of situations.

This lesson covers all or part of the following Adobe Photoshop CS5 ACE Exam objectives:

- Topic A
    - Objective 2.3 Given a scenario, use Opacity and fill controls in the Layers panel to achieve a desired effect (options include ability to vary Opacity/Fill of multiple layers).
    - Objective 8.1 Given a scenario, use the Mixer Brush and its options properly.
    - Objective 8.2 Given a scenario, adjust Bristle Tip brush settings appropriately.
    - Objective 8.3 Given a scenario, choose and use the proper method of choosing color (options include HUD Color Picker, Eyedropper tool with color ring, Swatches panel, Color panel, and the Color Picker).
    - Objective 8.5 Create and use gradients and patterns.

TOPIC A
Paint on an Image

You worked with layers. Now, you may want to enhance the images in the layers by painting on them. In this topic, you will paint on an image.

Images with plain and solid colors may sometimes look dull and boring. Painting on images with a slightly darker or lighter shade will add a natural effect to it. This will enhance the image and make it look distinctive.

Fill

A *fill* is a property that is applied to the inside of a shape, path, layer, or a selection. A fill can be a solid color, gradient, or pattern. A *gradient* fill is a gradual blend between two or more colors. You can apply a solid fill to an object using the **Paint Bucket** tool and a gradient fill using the **Gradient** tool available in the **Tools** panel.

The **Gradient** tool provides several gradient options.

Gradient Option	Description
Linear gradient	Flows in a straight line.
Radial gradient	Flows in a circular pattern.
Angle gradient	Flows in a counterclockwise sweep around a starting point.
Reflected gradient	Uses symmetric linear gradients on two sides of the starting point.
Diamond gradient	Starts from a point and goes outward in a diamond pattern. The corner of the diamond pattern is defined by the endpoint.

The SWATCHES Panel

Swatches are a collection of preset colors available in the **SWATCHES** panel. They are displayed as a grid of colors in small squares. You can add to or subtract from the default swatch set and load any saved sets.

There are several commands available on the **SWATCHES** panel options menu using which you can create a color swatch, and reset, load, save, and replace swatches. You can also change the display of the thumbnails to small or large thumbnails, along with the names of the colors.

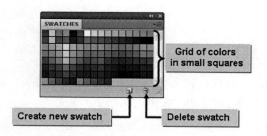

Figure 6-1: Grid of colors displayed in the SWATCHES panel.

Brushes

Brushes can be utilized to simulate the effect of painting with a real paintbrush. Using the **BRUSH** panel, you can select a standard brush and specify the settings to create a custom brush. A custom brush is created by specifying the attributes in the **BRUSH** panel. You can select a brush tip from the **Brush Preset** picker, modify it using various options, and apply different effects to the brush tip. The custom brush thus created can be saved and loaded using the **BRUSH** panel or the **Brush Preset** picker.

Some of the attributes that can be applied to the brush tip using the **BRUSH** panel are described in the table.

Attribute	*Enables You To*
Brush Tip Shape	Set the brush shape, diameter, angle, roundness, hardness, and spacing.
Shape Dynamics	Ascertain the dynamics of brush marks in a brush stroke.
Scattering	Apply brush strokes with a scattered effect.
Texture	Apply brush strokes with a pattern so it looks like it is painted on a texture.
Dual Brush	Combine two brush tips.
Color Dynamics	Control the variation in the color of a stroke.
Other Dynamics	Paint the color of a stroke that fades off gradually. For example, dark shade at the beginning of a stroke gradually fading off to a lighter shade.

Patterns

A *pattern* adds a repetitive or tiled effect to a selected area. Photoshop provides predefined patterns that are available in the pattern library. You can create patterns using drawing tools such as **Pen, Freeform Pen, Pencil, Brush,** and **Shapes.** You can edit existing patterns using various options in Photoshop and apply different effects to them. The custom pattern can be saved for future use using the **Preset Manager.**

The Brush Tool Options Bar

When you select the **Brush** tool, the Options bar displays settings that allow you to select a predefined tool, brush type, and painting mode. You can select a predefined brush tip from the preset picker, specify its size, or create a brush preset. In addition, you can set the color transparency of the stroke, specify how quickly the paint is applied, and enable airbrush effects. By enabling airbrush, you can apply gradual tones to an image.

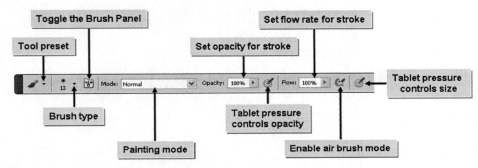

Figure 6-2: The various options displayed in the Brush tool Options bar.

The Tool Preset Feature

The Tool Preset feature allows you to save and reuse the settings of most tools. You can use the **Create new tool preset** button to create a preset. The commands on the **TOOL PRESETS** panel options menu allow you to load or replace tool presets in the Photoshop Presets folder. You can save the changes made to a new or an existing preset file using the **Save Tool Presets** command. You can also use the **Reset Tool Presets** command to restore the presets to their default settings.

The Mixer Brush Tool

The **Mixer Brush** tool allows you to create natural and realistic painting effects on images. It allows you to blend colors with the underlying colors in the layer. The brush settings allow you to control the wetness, the paint load rate, and the mixing rate of brush and layer colors. You can also specify whether the brush must be refilled with paint or cleaned, or both refilled and cleaned after every painting stroke.

Bristle Tips

Photoshop CS5 allows maximum control over the stroke characteristics of brushes with bristle tips. These brushes allow you to define properties such as space, density, length, stiffness, thickness, angle, and spacing of bristles. The bristle brush preview provides a visual representation of the movement of the bristles when the brush is used to paint. This preview can be enabled or disabled using the **BRUSH** panel.

How to Paint on an Image

 ACA: 4.6f Demonstrate knowledge of color blending. (Notes for item writers: Use the Mixer Brush to define multiple colors on a single tip and mix and blend them into the underlying colors on your canvas, or use a dry brush to blend the colors into your photo to create a beautiful painting.)

Procedure Reference: Create a Swatch

To create a swatch:

1. In the **Tools** panel, click the **Set foreground color** icon.
2. In the **Color Picker (Foreground Color)** dialog box, type the values in the text boxes.
   - In the **R** text box, type the desired value for red.
   - In the **G** text box, type the desired value for green.
   - In the **B** text box, type the desired value for blue.
3. Select the **SWATCHES** panel.
4. Add a new swatch to the **SWATCHES** panel.
   - Click the **Create new swatch of foreground color** button or;
   - In the **SWATCHES** panel, in the last row, in the gray area to the right of the last color swatch, place the mouse pointer and click to add the new swatch to the **SWATCHES** panel.
5. Name the created swatch.
   a. From the **SWATCHES** panel options menu, choose **New Swatch.**
   b. In the **Color Swatch Name** dialog box, in the **Name** text box, type a name for the swatch and click **OK.**
6. Hold down **Ctrl** and click to set or change the background color.
7. Hold down **Alt** and click to delete a swatch.

Procedure Reference: Create a Tool Preset

To create a tool preset:

1. In the **Tools** panel, select a tool.
2. On the Options bar, set the desired options.
3. Display the **New Tool Preset** dialog box.
   - Click the **Tool Preset** button located to the left of the Options bar and then click the **Create new tool preset** button or;
   - Choose **Window→Tool Presets** to display the **Tool Presets** panel and then click the **Create new tool preset** button.

 The **New Tool Preset** dialog box can also be displayed by choosing **New Tool Preset** from the panel options menu.

4. In the **New Tool Preset** dialog box, in the **Name** text box, type a name and click **OK.**

Procedure Reference: Paint Shadows on a Layer

To paint shadows on a new layer:

1. Select a layer on which you want to paint shadows.

2. Select the desired color for the shadow.

3. Select the **Brush** tool.

4. On the Options bar, specify the settings.

    a. From the **Brush Preset** picker, select the desired brush size.

      ● Drag the **Size** slider to set the desired brush size or;

      ● Double-click in the **Size** text box and type a value to set the brush size.

    b. Click the **Set to enable airbrush capabilities** button.

    c. In the **Flow** text box, specify a flow value.

5. In the document window, drag along the image to which you want to apply the paint shadows.

Procedure Reference: Paint with the Mixer Brush Tool

To paint with the **Mixer Brush** tool:

1. Select the **Mixer Brush** tool.

2. Select the foreground or background color.

3. On the Options bar, specify the settings.

    ● Specify the size of the brush.

      a. From the **Brush Preset** picker, select the desired brush size.

      b. Double-click in the **Size** text box, type a value for the brush size or drag the **Size** slider to set the desired brush size.

> You can also select the size and the brush tip using the **BRUSH PRESETS** panel.

    ● From the **Current brush load** drop-down list, select an option to load or remove the fill color.

    ● From the **Preset** pop-up menu, select an option to apply combinations of dry, wet, moist, and to load as well.

    ● In the **Wet** text box, type a value or click the arrow beside the text box and drag the slider to specify the value to control the wetness.

    ● In the **Load** text box, type a value or click the arrow beside the text box and drag the slider to specify the amount of paint load rate.

    ● In the **Mix** text box, type a value or click the arrow beside the text box and drag the slider to specify the value to control the mixing rate of brush and layer colors.

    ● Check the **Sample All Layers** check box to pick colors from all the visible layers.

    ● In the **Flow** text box, specify a flow value.

4. Click and drag on an image to paint.

ACTIVITY 6-1
Painting on an Image

Data Files:

Color Sample Card.psd

Before You Begin:

1. Navigate to the C:\084384Data\Enhancing Images with Paint and Filters folder and open the Color Sample Card.psd document.

2. Set the zoom percentage of the document to 18.

Scenario:

You set the background of the cover page in sky blue color; however, you realize that the cover page can be enhanced by adding clouds to the sky background. You feel that this will lend a realistic look to the front page.

---

1. Create a layer called *Cloud 1.*

   a. In the **LAYERS** panel, verify that the Group 1 folder is expanded.

   b. Scroll down, select the Home layer, and click the **Create a new layer** button to create a layer.

   c. Rename the layer as *Cloud 1*

---

2. Draw a cloud on the sky background.

   a. In the **Tools** panel, select the **Brush** tool.

   b. On the Options bar, click the **Click to open the Brush Presets picker** drop-down arrow.

   c. In the Preset picker, in the first row, click the second last brush type from the right, to select it.

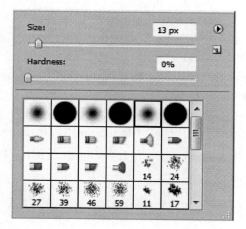

---

d. In the **Size** text box, click and drag over the value, type *500* and then press **Enter.**

e. In the **Tools** panel, click the **Default Foreground and Background Colors** button.

f. Click the **Switch Foreground and Background Colors** button.

g. On the Options bar, in the **Opacity** text box, double-click, type *55* and then press **Enter.**

h. Click at the point of intersection of the 2200-pixel mark on the horizontal ruler and the 700-pixel mark on the vertical ruler.

i. Click at the point of intersection of the 2350-pixel mark on the horizontal ruler and the 650-pixel mark on the vertical ruler.

j. Click at the point of intersection of the 2400-pixel mark on the horizontal ruler and the 700-pixel mark on the vertical ruler.

3. Create another cloud by duplicating the existing one.

a. In the **Tools** panel, select the **Move** tool.

b. Choose **Layer→Duplicate Layer.**

c. In the **Duplicate Layer** dialog box, in the **As** text box, type *Cloud 2* and click **OK.**

d. Click anywhere in the cloud and drag it to place it at the top-left corner between the roof and the text.

e. Save the file as *My Color Sample Card* in the PSD format.

OPTIONAL ACTIVITY 6-2
Painting with the Mixer Brush Tool

Data Files:

Paint Interior.psd, Flower.psd

Before You Begin:

Navigate to the C:\084384Data\Enhancing Images with Paint and Filters folder and open the Paint Interior.psd and Flower.psd files.

Scenario:

Your colleague has created an interior of a room with the wall painted with a particular pattern. You are required to create a color shade that matches the pattern on the wall. So, you need to mix two colors to bring the color and the pattern in the paint can.

---

1.   Specify the desired settings to create a color shade.

   a.   Switch to the Paint Interior.psd file.

   b.   In the **Tools** panel, click the **Set foreground color** box.

   c.   In the **Color Picker (Foreground Color)** dialog box, in the # text box, double-click and type *954d1d* and then click **OK.**

   d.   From the **Brush** tool flyout, select the **Mixer Brush** tool.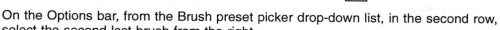

   e.   On the Options bar, from the Brush preset picker drop-down list, in the second row, select the second last brush from the right.

   f.   In the **Size** text box, click and drag over the value, type *80* and then press **Enter.**

   g.   Click the Application bar to hide the menu.

   h.   From the **Blending brush combination** drop-down list, select **Very Wet, Light Mix.**

---

2.   Paint inside the paint can to create a color shade that matches the wall.

   a.   In the **LAYERS** panel, select the Paint layer.

   b.   Hold down **Ctrl** and select the layer thumbnail of the Paint layer.

   c.   Set the zoom percentage of the document to *200*

   d.   In the document window, scroll to the left and up to view the selection.

   e.   Inside the selection, click and drag the brush diagonally from the left to the right to create strokes until you cover the entire selection.

   f.   Choose **Select→Deselect.**

   g.   Set the zoom percentage to *35*

---

3.   Transfer the flower vase onto the table of the interior design file.

a.   In the **Tools** panel, select the **Move** tool.

b.   Open the Flower.psd file as a floating window and close the window.

c.   Click the flower vase image and drag it to place it on the table.

d.   Choose **Edit→Free Transform.**

e.   On the Options bar, specify the value for **W** and **H** as *3*

f.   Similarly, specify the values for **X** and **Y** as *496* and *333* respectively.

g.   Click the **Commit transform (Return)** button.

h.   Save the file as *My Paint Interior* in the PSD format.

i.   Close the file.

TOPIC B
Apply Filter Effects

You enhanced images by painting on it. Another way of enhancing images is by applying filter effects to images. In this topic, you will apply filter effects.

The filters available in Photoshop endow you with the ability to enhance images without spending a lot of time on creating it. By combining the filters available in Photoshop, you can create a nearly endless variety of effects.

Filters

A *filter* is a feature that allows you to apply special effects and change the appearance of images. These special effects are listed with the sample content in a central location. In Photoshop, you can preview filter effects on images and then apply them using the **Filter Gallery.** You can alter, retouch, or polish images, and give them different lighting effects using filters. You can also apply a filter to the active layer or selection in an image.

Filter Effects

In Photoshop, filters are classified into many groups based on the effect they have on an image. Filter groups include **Artistic, Blur,** and **Texture.** Each filter group contains individual filters that apply a certain effect to the image. Some of the individual filters are **Sponge** that simulates sponge painting; **Grain** that adds texture to an image by simulating different types of grains; and **Blur** that softens the entire image or a selection.

Original Image   Image with Sponge filter effect applied   Image with Grain filter effect applied

Figure 6-3: Different filter effects applied to an object.

The Browse Filters Online Command
The **Browse Filters Online** command on the **Filter** menu will take you to the Adobe website from which you can choose other filter effects that are not available in the Adobe Photoshop CS5 application.

Filter Effects and Their Uses
Filter effects in Photoshop are used to apply special effects to images and they can be applied using the commands on the **Filter** menu. Using these ready-made filters, you can create realistic textures and stunning text effects.

Filter	Description
Artistic	Used to obtain art effects that resemble natural and traditional artistic creations created with different types of brushes, strokes, and styles of painting, colored papers, posterized effects, and much more. This is also used to create collages or typography.
Blur	Used to apply various effects such as smoothening the hard edges of an image, creating a hazy effect, creating a movement of an object, creating a depth of field effect, softening portions of an image, creating special effects, and much more.
Brush Strokes	Used to give a traditional fine art effect using different brush strokes and ink effects.
Distort	Used to distort images by applying effects such as 3D and reshaping. This filter requires high memory for smooth working.
Noise	Used to add or remove noise. It can be used to remove dust particles, scratches, or problem areas. This filter also helps blend a selection with the surrounding pixels, and can be used to create textures.
Pixelate	The commands on this submenu are used to combine neighboring pixels of related color values to create blocks of color that adds effects to an image.
Render	Used to create clouds, 3-D shapes, refraction patterns, and simulated light reflections in images.
Sharpen	Used to sharpen blurred images or soft edges by increasing the contrast of the adjacent pixels.
Sketch	Used to create artistic effects such as hand-drawn artwork by adding textures.
Stylize	Used to create an impressionistic or painted effect on a selected portion of an image.
Texture	Used to give different kinds of textures, such as sand, paper, mosaic tiles, stained glass effects, and more on images. These textures add depth to images.
Video	Used to smoothen moving images captured on videos using the **De-Interlace** command and to restrict a gamut of colors for television by using the **NTSC colors** command.
Other	Used to create customized filters.
Digimarc	Used to add digital watermarks to images for copyright purposes.

The Filter Gallery

The **Filter Gallery** lists the available filters that you can apply to an image. It also allows you to use more than one filter on an image. Using the **Filter Gallery** dialog box, you can preview how the filter will be applied to the image. In addition, you can view thumbnails that show the function of each filter, and rearrange and change filter settings. The filter settings vary based on the selected filter. By clicking the eye icon in the lower-right section of the **Filter Gallery** dialog box, you can view the original image without the filter effect.

How to Apply Filter Effects

Procedure Reference: Apply Filter Effects

To apply filter effects:

1. Select the layer to which the filter effect is to be applied.
2. Choose **Filter** and then choose the desired filter effect.
3. In the dialog box that is displayed, adjust the desired settings.
4. Click **OK.**

Procedure Reference: Apply a Filter Using the Filter Gallery

To apply a filter using the **Filter Gallery:**

1. Open the required Photoshop file.
2. Choose **Filter→Filter Gallery.**
3. Select a filter name and expand the category to display the thumbnail list.
4. Click the desired thumbnail and apply the desired settings.
5. Click **OK.**

ACTIVITY 6-3
Applying Filter Effects

Data Files:

My Color Sample Card.psd, Shades.png

Before You Begin:

The My Color Sample Card.psd is open.

Scenario:

Your supervisor did an initial review of the color sample card design and gave some suggestions for improvement. With this feedback, you decide to make modifications by applying effects such as adding texture behind the shades to give the card the appearance of a handmade paper. Also, to make the logo more prominent, you will try adding an effect that offers greater distinction.

---

1. Apply the blur filter effect to the cloud.

    a. In the **LAYERS** panel, select the Cloud 1 layer.

    b. Choose **Filter→Blur→Gaussian Blur.**

    c. In the **Gaussian Blur** dialog box, in the **Radius** text box, type *50* and click **OK.**

    d. In the **LAYERS** panel, in the **Opacity** text box, double-click, type *70* and then press **Enter.**

    e. Select the Cloud 2 layer.

    f. Choose **Filter→Gaussian Blur.**

    g. In the **LAYERS** panel, for the Cloud 1 layer, in the **Opacity** text box, double-click, type *70* and then press **Enter.**

---

2. Import color shades into the color sample card.

    a. Open the Shades.png file from the Enhancing Images with Paint and Filters folder.

    b. Display the document as a floating window and move the Shades image to the color sample card document.

    c. Choose **Edit→Free Transform.**

    d. On the Options bar, specify values for **X** and **Y** as *4222.5* and *1401* respectively.

    e. Click the **Commit transform (Return)** button.

---

3. Apply the handmade paper effect as a background for the shades using the filter effect.

    a. Scroll to the right of the document.

    b. In the **LAYERS** panel, scroll down and select the Cloud 2 layer.

    c. Create a layer and name it *Filter*

    d.   In the **Tools** panel, select the **Rectangular Marquee** tool.

    e.   Click at the point of intersection of the 2800-pixel mark on the horizontal ruler and the 0-pixel mark on the vertical ruler and drag to the point of intersection of the 5600-pixel mark on the horizontal ruler and the 2800-pixel mark on the vertical ruler.

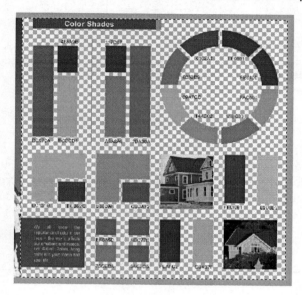

    f.   Select the **Paint Bucket** tool.

    g.   Click inside the selection.

    h.   Choose **Filter→Texture→Texturizer.**

    i.   In the **Texturizer (100%)** dialog box, in the third section, from the **Texture** drop-down list, select **Sandstone.**

    j.   In the **Scaling** text box, double-click and type *80*

    k.   In the **Relief** text box, double-click, type *8* and then click **OK.**

    l.   Deselect the selection.

    m.   Save and close the file.

Lesson 6 Follow-up

In this lesson, you enhanced images by applying colors and filters. By enhancing images, you can add more visual appeal to an image and make it look more realistic.

1. **Which brush type and mode do you think you will use often in your work environment?**

2. **When selecting filter types, which effects do you think will be most beneficial to you? Why?**

7 Exploring Image Modes and Color Adjustments

Lesson Time: 15 minutes

Lesson Objectives:

In this lesson, you will identify the characteristics of various image modes and color adjustment options.

You will:

● Explore Grayscale and Bitmap modes.

● Apply color adjustments.

Introduction

You enhanced images with paints and filters. You may now find the need to understand the similarities and differences in image types or modes to get the most from Photoshop images. In this lesson, you will explore the different image modes and color adjustments.

A black and white portrait reminds us of old days and of the limited choices people had even if it came to capturing sweet memories on a black and white camera. Today, this is not the case. Not only do we have a wide array of gadgets that capture our memories on beautiful and colorful portraits, but we also have choices that allow us to make a display of our captured memories on a variety of mediums such as the web. From a mere black and white combination, colors are now being defined as a means to enhance the appearance of images.

Image modes come in a variety of options and blends. The color mode you choose determines the number and range of colors that can be displayed in an image. In order to choose the appropriate color mode for your image, you need to first understand how each mode works.

This lesson covers all or part of the following Adobe Visual Communication using Photoshop CS5 objectives:

● Topic B

  ■ Objective 2.4a: Identify the differences between RGB and CMYK.

  ■ Objective 2.4f: Demonstrate knowledge of how to select the appropriate color modes for web, print, and video.

- Objective 4.4b: Identify adjustment menu tools that are used for adjusting tone.
- Objective 4.4c: Identify advanced adjustment tools and when to use them.
- Objective 4.4e: Demonstrate knowledge of how to match, mix, and replace color by using a specific set of tools.
- Objective 4.4f: Demonstrate knowledge of how to adjust hue and saturation.

TOPIC A
Explore Grayscale and Bitmap Modes

While working in Photoshop, you may need to characterize and work with image modes based on some specific needs. Before you begin, however, you should be in a position to distinguish the technical differences in different kinds of black and white images. In this topic, you will explore Grayscale and Bitmap modes that deal with black and white images.

There may be occasions when you need to use black and white images and enhance their attributes. However, while working with images in Photoshop, it becomes necessary to know the differences between grayscale and bitmap image modes in order to incorporate black and white colors in images using different methods.

Bitmap

A *bitmap* is a file format of an image that has single 1-bit channels that result in two available shades of brightness: black and white. The size of a bitmap image depends on the number of pixels it contains. Pixels are tiny dots of color that result in an image. The greater the number of pixels, the larger the file size. Bitmap images that are enlarged beyond their original size become distorted and out of focus. A bitmap image is resolution dependent. Bitmap resolution is determined by dots per inch (dpi) or pixels per inch (ppi).

Compressed Bitmap Image Formats

The compressed bitmap image formats are Joint Photographic Experts Group (JPEG), Graphics Interchange Format (GIF), and Portable Networks Graphics Format (PNG). JPEG is designed for compressing grayscale or 24-bit color images and supports up to 16 million colors. GIF is an 8-bit format and supports up to 256 colors. PNG has better compression than GIF, supports gray scale and 24-bit color images, and can support millions of colors.

Grayscale

Grayscale images are 1-channel, 8-bit images that result in 255 brightness levels, ranging from 0 or pure black to 255 or pure white. Grayscale is a more accurate term for black and white photos. Although they are printed using only black ink, the pixels in the version you edit on the screen are levels of gray, with the conversion to a black and white halftone occurring during the printing process.

Duotone

A *duotone* is a type of image that is printed in two colors. It is a 1-channel, 8-bit image like a grayscale image. However, it differs in the way in which the image is printed. The duotone mode allows you to assign two, three, or four inks, namely, duotone, tritone, or quadtone, to print certain tones of the image in different colors. Photoshop's duotone mode is also commonly used for creating sepia-toned prints. Sepia toning is a treatment given to photographs to restore its original quality, to give it a warmer tone, and to enhance its appearance.

ACTIVITY 7-1
Exploring Grayscale and Bitmap Modes

Scenario:

You want the front cover design of the color sample card to be printed in black and white properly. To ensure this, you need to be familiar with the different modes available in Photoshop.

---

1. **Which image does not contain any gray level?**

    a) PNG

    b) JPEG

    c) BMP

    d) GIF

---

2. **True or False? Duotone is a 1-channel, 8-bit image.**

    ___ True

    ___ False

TOPIC B
Apply Color Adjustments

You explored Grayscale and Bitmap modes. Now, you may need to choose color modes appropriately to suit your needs. In this topic, you will apply color adjustments.

At times you will not be satisfied with the existing color of an image or background, especially when you import images from another application. You might have chosen the right color, but you still feel it does not match with the background. A little fine tuning will be required to get the desired result. Using Photoshop and its various color adjustments options, you can easily achieve the image color you want.

Pixel Depth

Pixel depth refers to the number of colors that can possibly be displayed on a screen. It determines how many numbers of bits are used to make a pixel. The greater the pixel depth, the more accurately the image is represented. A simple formula based on the pixel depth determines the number of colors or shades.

Determining the Number of Colors

The formula for determining the number of colors based on the pixel depth is $2^{pixel\ depth}$. For example, a 1-bit image has a total of 2 shades, because 2^1 is 2. An 8-bit image has a total of 256 shades, because 2^8 is 256.

Photoshop Modes

All Photoshop modes, from the simplest to the most complex, differ only in terms of the number of channels and the pixel depth per channel. The complexity and file size of an image increase or decrease based on the number of channels and the pixel depth.

Color Mode

Definition:

Color mode is the mode that is used for displaying and printing images. It determines an image's file size and the number of colors and channels. The color mode is based on the color models used by images during publishing.

Example:

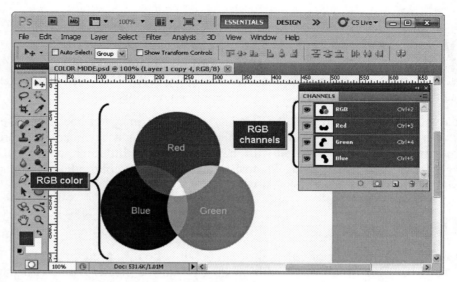

Figure 7-1: Three channels representing colors—R, G, and B.

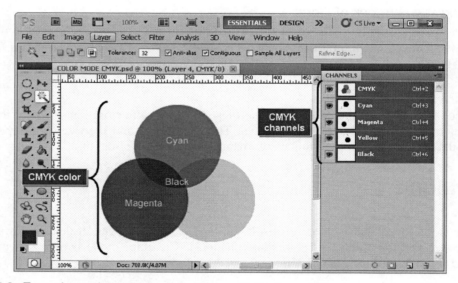

Figure 7-2: Four channels representing colors—C, M, Y, and K.

Different Color Modes

Photoshop images can be classified into different color modes based on the color information they contain. Some of these modes are specific to black and white images.

The following table describes the various color modes in Photoshop.

Color Mode	Uses
RGB Color	Three channels to represent color. Each color component—red, green, and blue—can use 256 shades. The RGB color mode is most commonly used for images distributed electronically. It is also used by monitors and scanners.
CMYK Color	Four channels to represent color. The color components are Cyan, Magenta, Yellow, and Black. The four channels result in over 4 billion available colors. This mode is used by printers.
Lab Color	Three channels to represent color. This color mode defines colors mathematically and is not device specific. The color components L, A, and B denote luminance component ranging from black to white, chromatic component ranging from green to red, and chromatic component ranging from blue to yellow respectively.
Indexed Color	A single channel to represent color. The bit depth can be set from 1 to 8 bits. A color table is used to determine the available colors.
Multichannel	256 levels of gray in each channel. It is used for specialized printing. Multichannel mode images support many file formats.
Bitmap	A single channel that results in two shades of brightness—black and white. This mode does not contain any intermediary gray levels. This mode is used for creating simple logos, line art, and special effects such as mezzotints.
Grayscale	A single 8-bit channel. This results in 256 brightness levels ranging from 0 (for pure black) to 255 (for pure white).
Duotone	A single 8-bit channel. This mode allows you to use two to four inks to print certain tones of the image in different colors. It is typically used to print tinted images and images with special ink requirements.

Color Modes for Different Output

Different color modes are used for web, print, and video. Use RGB for web, video, and for any screen display, and use CMYK for printing. In Photoshop, you may choose to convert color profiles per the need. For example, you may want to convert a RGB color image to a CMYK profile. For this purpose, you may use **The Convert To Profile** command. This command can be used to convert the image color values of a specified color space. Other commands that are used for this purpose are the **Assign Profile** and **Convert To Profile** commands. These commands are useful either when you want to convert an image to another profile after it has been opened or when an image is viewed in an inappropriate color space. Incorrect usage of these commands will result in a color profile that does not represent the intended appearance of an image.

Primary Colors

Red, green, and blue are referred to as the three additive primary colors, because they add together to create white when projected from a light source such as light bulbs or phosphors of your computer monitor. However, you cannot use RGB color for printing because red, green, and blue inks darken when they overlap instead of becoming brighter.

Difference Between RGB and CMYK Color Modes

RGB is a color mode that defines colors by their red, green, and blue components. Each pixel comprises these components with an intensity value ranging from 0 to 255. When combined, the result is a full-color image. Red, green, and blue are often referred to as the three "additive primary colors." The maximum intensity of the three colors together generates the color white. RGB is used for publishing images on the web.

CMYK color mode assigns each pixel a percentage value for each process ink. While the lightest colors are assigned small percentages, the darkest colors are assigned high percentages of process ink colors. Printers use the subtractive primary colors, cyan, magenta, yellow, and black, for ink colors. The colors are represented by the letters C, M, Y, and K, respectively.

Features of Indexed Colors

Indexed color images are often saved in the CompuServe GIF format for use on web pages. Due to its smaller file size, the transfer rate of these images is faster. However, the limit of 256 colors makes smooth color transitions and realistic display of color photos difficult. Therefore, indexed color is best suited for color illustrations.

Color Separation

Although color inkjet printers use cyan, magenta, yellow, black, and occasionally other additional inks, most color inkjet printer drivers are optimized for printing RGB images. Therefore, you should not convert the image from RGB to CMYK in Photoshop. However, during commercial printing or while using more expensive printers that use the PostScript® printing language, you should convert the image to CMYK. This process is called color separation, because for commercial printing, the four ink colors are printed separately on a press. To perform the conversion, you can choose the CMYK color mode on the **Mode** submenu.

Application of Lab Color

The Lab color mode is used internally by Photoshop when converting colors between image modes such as from RGB to CMYK. It is also used by a color management software that modifies images automatically, so that they appear the same on different printers and monitors. Also, because it separates luminance from color, Lab color is useful for editing image lightness without modifying the color.

Color Adjustments

The lightness, darkness, and contrast of an image can be adjusted by applying the various options on the **Adjustments** submenu. The adjustments commands can be used to correct image blemishes, dust particles, or other types of flaws. You can opt to adjust a particular area or the entire image.

Some of the Color Adjustments Commands

The following table describes some of the color adjustments commands available on the **Adjustments** submenu of the **Image** menu.

Command	Allows You To
Brightness/Contrast	Adjust the tonal range of an image by increasing or decreasing the tonal values by applying highlights on images.
Levels	Adjust the color balance by distributing pixels evenly.
Curves	Adjust image tones up to 14 different points that range from shadows to midtones to highlights.
Exposure	Adjust tones in images, especially 8-bit and 16-bit images. This is based on calculating the linear color space in an image.
Vibrance	Increase the saturation of less-saturated colors and prevent over saturation of colors in an image.
Color Balance	Correct the color distribution of an image by changing the complete mixture of colors in an image.
Black & White	Convert a color image to a grayscale image. It also allows you to tint the grayscale image.
Photo Filter	Adjust the color balance of the light captured through the camera lens. This command also allows you to choose a preset to adjust the hue level in an image.
Invert	Invert the colors in an image.
Posterize	Specify the tonal levels of each channel in an image to map to the closest level. This is mainly used to apply special effects to an image.
Threshold	Convert the grayscale images or color images to high-contrast black and white images by specifying a threshold value. Pixels that are lighter than the threshold are converted to white and pixels that are darker than the threshold are converted to black.
Gradient Map	Map the grayscale values of equal ranges to the colors of the gradient fill of an image.
Selective Color	Perform color correction on selective colors in an image without affecting the other colors of an image.
Shadows/Highlights	Brighten shadow areas or darken highlights and automatically mask the areas based on brightness, so that only those tonal ranges are affected. The default value for Shadows/Highlights is 35%.
Variations	Add color tones to areas of an image such as shadows, midtones, and highlights.

Command	Allows You To
Equalize	Distribute the pixel values of brightness in an image evenly so that the brightest values represent white and the darkest values represent black. This is mainly used to brighten dark images.
Hue/Saturation	Adjust the hue, saturation, and brightness of a selected image area or an entire image.
Match Color	Match the color from one image to another, from one layer to another, and from one selected image area to another selection of the same or different image. This option is also used to neutralize colors.
Replace Color	Create a mask temporarily over a selected image area and then replace the same color.
Channel Mixer	Modify the color channel by using the mixture of the existing color channels in an image. This option also converts the color image to grayscale by using the **Black and White** command.
Desaturate	Convert a color image to a grayscale image without changing its color mode.
Dodge	Use the **Dodge** tool to lighten the exposed area of a photograph. Using this tool, you can ascertain color information and brightness. You can also decrease contrast or increase brightness to reflect the blend color.
Burn	Use the **Burn** tool to darken the exposed area of a photograph. Using this tool, you can ascertain color information and darken the base color. You can also increase contrast or decrease brightness to reflect the blend color.

The ADJUSTMENTS Layer

You can also apply color adjustments using the options in the **ADJUSTMENTS** panel. Applying color adjustments with the **ADJUSTMENTS** panel is more flexible because it does not change the color permanently, and you can always delete it from the **LAYERS** panel.

How to Apply Color Adjustments

Procedure Reference: Apply Color Adjustments to an Image

To apply color adjustments to an image:

1. Choose **Image→Adjustments.**
2. From the **ADJUSTMENTS** submenu, choose the desired command.
3. Specify the desired settings
4. Click **OK.**

Procedure Reference: Apply Color Adjustments Using the Hue/Saturation Option

To apply color adjustments using the **Hue/Saturation** option:

1. Select the appropriate image, if necessary.
2. Choose **Image→Adjustments→Hue/Saturation.**
3. If necessary, check the **Colorize** check box to apply color adjustments to the image according to the chosen foreground color.
4. Adjust the hue/saturation by specifying the desired settings.
   - From the **Preset** drop-down list, select the desired option either to use the default settings or to customize it.
   - In the **Hue** text box, type the desired value to increase or decrease the color of an image.
   - In the **Saturation** text box, type the desired value to increase or decrease the saturation level of the hue.
   - In the **Lightness** text box, type the desired value to set the lightness for a specified range of colors in an image.
5. Click **OK.**

ACTIVITY 7-2
Applying Color Adjustments

Data Files:

Color Sample Card.psd

Before You Begin:

Navigate to the C:\084384Data\Exploring Image Modes and Color Adjustments folder and open the Color Sample Card.psd file.

Scenario:

You are almost done with the color sample card and you realize that one of the home images looks a bit dull and faded. You decide to correct the image to suit the shade's background. Once the minor adjustments are done, you want to send a copy of the card to the client to get feedback. You realize that the feedback may result in slight modifications. You decide to keep a copy of the file intact with the original layers.

---

1. Apply color adjustments to the home image.

   a. In the **LAYERS** panel, select Layer 1.

   b. Select the **Rectangular Marquee** tool.

   c. Set the zoom percentage to *30*

   d. In the document window, scroll to the right so that the blue house image is visible.

   e. Click and drag from the upper-left corner of the house image diagonally down to the bottom-right corner to select the entire image.

   f. Choose **Image→Adjustments→Hue/Saturation.**

   g. In the **Hue/Saturation** dialog box, in the **Hue** text box, double-click and type *3* and then press **Tab.**

   h. In the **Saturation** text box, type *58* and then press **Tab.**

   i. In the **Lightness** text box, type *4* and then click **OK.**

   j. Deselect the selection.

k.   Save the file as ***My Color Sample Card*** in the PSD format.

2.   Save the file as Client Copy.psd in the PSD format.

a.   Choose **Layer→Flatten Image.**

b.   In the **LAYERS** panel, observe that the image is flattened and the layer is locked.

c.   Save the file as ***Client Copy*** in the PSD format.

d.   Close the Client Copy.psd file.

Lesson 7 Follow-up

In this lesson, you explored image modes and color adjustments. Selecting the correct image mode and color adjustment in Photoshop enables you to obtain quality output for an image.

1. **In what situations will you prefer using the grayscale color mode and bitmap images?**

2. **In previous projects, what errors did you encounter as a result of picking the wrong image mode?**

8 Saving Images for Web and Print

Lesson Time: 45 minutes

Lesson Objectives:

In this lesson, you will save images for web and print.

You will:

● Save images for use in print applications.

● Save images for the web.

● Save images as PDF files.

Introduction

You explored the various image modes and applied color adjustments to images. Now, you may want to save the images in different formats so that they can be used for either print or web. In this lesson, you will save completed images for web and print applications.

A file format that suits print might not necessarily meet the requirements for the web. To get the best possible output for various applications, you may need to save the document in different file formats. Understanding the different file formats and their usage ensures that you get the best output for a specific medium.

This lesson covers all or part of the following Adobe Visual Communication using Photoshop CS5 objectives:

● Topic A

■ Objective 2.1c: Identify appropriate image formats for web, video, photos, print, PowerPoint, or Word.

■ Objective 2.1e: Demonstrate knowledge of image optimization with regards to preparing images for web, video, or print.

■ Objective 2.5e: Identify the most appropriate image type to use in a variety of situations.

■ Objective 3.3c: Demonstrate knowledge of how to optimize images for print and web.

■ Objective 3.3d: Demonstrate knowledge of creating contact sheets and picture packages.

- ■ Objective 3.3e: Demonstrate knowledge of how to save print dialog settings as presets.

- ● Topic B

  - ■ Objective 2.1c: Identify appropriate image formats for web, video, photos, print, PowerPoint, or Word.

  - ■ Objective 2.1e: Demonstrate knowledge of image optimization with regards to preparing images for web, video, or print.

  - ■ Objective 2.5e: Identify the most appropriate image type to use in a variety of situations.

  - ■ Objective 3.3c: Demonstrate knowledge of how to optimize images for print and web.

TOPIC A
Save Images for Print

You applied color adjustments to images. Now, you may want to save the images in a format that has the optimum quality and file size for the print medium. In this topic, you will save images for use in print applications.

While working on images, you need to ensure that the images look good when they are used for commercial printing. The print media will require a different quality of output from web. By optimizing images for print, you can ensure a proper output of images.

File Formats for Print Applications

Files for print applications are typically saved in Tagged Image File Format (TIFF) or Encapsulated PostScript (EPS) file format. Photoshop images that are designed for printing purposes are also saved in these formats. TIFF supports only raster graphics and can be used on both Windows and Mac platforms. EPS, on the other hand, supports both vector and raster graphics, and is used to transfer PostScript images between applications.

EPS and TIFF File Formats

EPS does not support layers, whereas TIFF generally does; but some applications cannot properly import layered TIFF files. Therefore, you should save the TIFF file without layers. This can be done by checking the **Layers** check box in the **Save As** dialog box.

The Save As a Copy Option

Photoshop provides you with an option to save a copy of a file. This is useful, especially when you save the file in the TIFF or EPS format because the original file with the layers intact will not be replaced when you save the file in a different format. This is important because you may need to return to the original file that includes layers, to make changes later.

Best Practice While Saving Images

While saving images in another format, it is best to have three versions of it. You can have a copy of the source file before making any changes to it, a copy of the file as a Photoshop (.psd) file so that it can be edited in Photoshop, and finally the file as it is saved in the desired format.

TIFF Options

When you save a Photoshop image in TIFF, you can use the **TIFF Options** dialog box to specify the settings for compression, compatibility, resolution, and transparency.

The following table describes the options to optimize an image for printing using the **TIFF Options** dialog box.

Component	*Used To*
Image Compression section	Compress an image to decrease the file size.
Pixel Order section	Specify the arrangement of pixel data (RGB channels).

Component	Used To
Byte Order section	Specify the platform (Windows or Macintosh) on which the file will be read. Most programs can read either byte orders.
Save Image Pyramid check box	Preserve multi-resolution information in an image when checked.
Save Transparency check box	Preserve the transparency as an alpha channel when checked.
Layer Compression section	Compress the data in each layer if layers are saved as TIFF files. There are three options available to compress a TIFF file, namely **RLE (faster saves, bigger files)**, **ZIP (slower saves, smaller files)**, and **Discard Layers and Save a Copy.**

The Print Commands

Photoshop provides a number of print commands that enable you to print documents.

The following table describes the various print commands.

Print Command	Description
Print	Displays the **Print** dialog box. This dialog box displays the printing, output, and color management options in Photoshop.
Print One Copy	Allows you to print only one copy of the file and does not display the **Print** dialog box.

Printing Photoshop Images

Photoshop images can be output to a variety of sources. When preparing to print images on a non-commercial local or network printer, Photoshop provides options to help control the printing of the images. By default, Photoshop prints a composite of visible layers. To print an individual layer, you need to hide the other layers and then choose the **Print** command.

Your monitor displays images using light, while a printer reproduces images using inks and pigments. As a result, the hard copy image can appear quite different. There are certain color management options displayed in the **Print** dialog box that can be used to increase the predictability of the printed image.

The Print Dialog Box

The **Print** dialog box contains various options that can be specified as presets and applied to a document before printing. The options in the dialog box allow you to preview, position, and scale the image, and specify the number of copies to be printed. You can also specify color management and output settings using this dialog box. It also allows you to set print options for printers and printer drivers. The preview options in the dialog box enable you to view the colors that will be printed, the out-of-range colors, and the white color in images. The **Done** button allows you to save the settings as presets.

The Print Settings Option

The **Print Settings** option in the **Print** dialog box allows you to set parameters, such as page orientation and size of margins, to determine the look of the printed output.

Contact Sheets

Contact sheets are pages that contain a group of images as thumbnail layouts on a single page. They help in printing different images in the same size on a single sheet for various purposes such as reducing the cost of color printing. The **Contact Sheet II** dialog box allows you to preview thumbnail layouts, choose a layout for the contact sheet by specifying the dimensions, resolution, and color mode, and specify thumbnail settings by selecting the position of images, space between images, and number of columns and rows of images per sheet.

Picture Packages

Picture packages are pages that contain layouts of multiple images or photographs on a single page. They are generally used to print multiple copies of the same images in the same size or in different sizes. In Photoshop, you can create different types of picture package layouts using the **Picture Package** command on the **File** menu. Using the **Picture Package** dialog box, you can not only choose from a variety of size and placement options to customize the package layout but also display copies of a single photograph. Additionally, you can scale the photographs to fit them correctly on a page using the **Edit Layout** button in the dialog box.

Figure 8-1: Images added to create a picture package.

How to Save Images for Print

Procedure Reference: Save a File for Print

To save a file for print:

1.   Open the required Photoshop file.
2.   Choose **File→Save As.**
3.   In the **Save As** dialog box, from the **Format** drop-down list, select the desired format.
4.   In the **Save Options** section, specify the desired settings.
     - Check the **As a Copy** check box to save a copy of the file and keep the current file open.
     - Check the **Alpha Channels** check box to save alpha channel information along with the image.
     - Check the **Layers** check box to preserve all the layers in the image.
5.   Click **Save.**
6.   In the dialog box for the selected format, mention the desired settings and click **OK.**

Procedure Reference: Save Print Presets

To save print presets:

1.   Open a Photoshop file.
2.   Choose **File→Print** to display the **Print** dialog box.
3.   From the **Printer** drop-down list, select the printer.
4.   In the **Copies** text box, type a number to specify the number of copies that need to be printed.
5.   If necessary, click the **Print Settings** button and specify the properties such as document size, type, quality, and more for the printed output.
6.   In the **Position** section, specify the desired settings.
     - Check the **Center Image** check box to position the image in the center or;
     - Specify values in the **Top** and **Left** text boxes.
7.   If necessary, from the **Units** drop-down list, select an option.
8.   In the **Scaled Print Size** section, specify the desired settings.
     - Check the **Scale to Fit Media** check box to position the image in the center or;
     - Specify the values in the **Scale, Height,** and **Width** text boxes.
9.   From the **Color Handling** drop-down list, select a color handling method according to the printer settings.
10. From the **Printer Profile** drop-down list, select an option.
11. If necessary, from the **Rendering Intent** drop-down list, select an option.
     - Select **Perceptual** to preserve the visual relationship between colors.
     - Select **Saturation** to produce vivid colors in an image at the expense of color accuracy.
     - Select **Relative Colorimetric** to compare the white of the source color space with the destination color space, and to change the colors accordingly.
     - Select **Absolute Colorimetric** to not change the colors that fall inside the destination gamut.

12. If necessary, from the **Proof Setup** drop-down list, select an option.

13. Click **Done** to save the specified options as presets.

Procedure Reference: Convert Images to the CMYK Profile

To convert an image to the CMYK profile:

1. Open an image in Photoshop.

2. Choose **Edit→Convert to Profile** to display the **Convert to Profile** dialog box.

3. In the **Destination Space** section, from the **Profile** drop-down list, select the color profile to which you want to convert the document's colors.

 The **Source Space** section displays the current working color space.

4. In the **Conversion Options** section, specify the desired settings.
   - From the **Engine** drop-down list, select a color management engine.
   - From the **Intent** drop-down list, select a rendering intent.

5. Click **OK.**

Procedure Reference: Create a Contact Sheet

To create a contact sheet:

1. Open the required images.

2. Choose **File→Automate→Contact Sheet II.**

3. In the **Contact Sheet II** dialog box, specify the images from the source area.
   - Select **Current Open Documents** to use the image that is in the current document or;
   - Select **Folder** to specify the folder in which the source images are placed.
     - Click the **Browse** button and in the **Browse For Folder** dialog box, navigate to the folder that is specified as the root folder for a project and click **OK.**
     - If necessary, check the **Include All Subfolders** check box to include images that are placed inside the subfolders.

4. In the **Document** section, specify the settings such as page size, resolution, and color mode.

 Check the **Flatten All Layers** check box to flatten all images and text on a single layer.

5. In the **Thumbnails** section, specify the desired settings.

    ● From the **Place** drop-down list, select an option to place the thumbnails across first or down first in a document or page.

    ● In the **Columns** and **Rows** text boxes, type a value to specify the number of columns and rows of images per sheet.

    ● Check the **Use Auto Spacing** check box to provide space automatically.

    ● In the **Vertical** text box, type a value to specify the space for vertical thumbnails.

    ● In the **Horizontal** text box, type a value to specify the space for horizontal thumbnails.

    ● Check the **Rotate For best Fit** check box to rotate the images, so they fit exactly on a contact sheet.

6. In the **Use Filename As Caption** section, select the appropriate option to label the thumbnails.

    ● From the **Font** drop-down list, select an option.

    ● From the **Font Size** drop-down list, select an option.

7. Click **OK** and view the output.

Procedure Reference: Create Picture Packages

To create picture packages:

1. Open the required images.

2. Choose **File→Automate→Picture Package.**

3. In the **Picture Package** dialog box, specify the settings.

    ● In the **Source Images** section, from the **Use** drop-down list, select an option.

      ■ Select **File** to specify the file in which the source images are placed.

      ■ Select **Folder** to specify the folder in which the source images are placed.

      ■ Select **Frontmost Documents** to use the image that is in the current document.

      ■ Click the **Browse** button and in the **Browse For Folder** dialog box, navigate to the folder that is specified as the root folder for a project and click **OK.**

      ■ Check the **Include All Subfolders** check box to include images that are placed inside subfolders.

    ● Add one or more images.

      ■ In the **Layout** section, click the placeholder of any preview layout and navigate to the file or folder to select an image or;

      ■ Drag an image from the file or folder to the placeholder.

    ● In the **Document** section, specify the settings such as page size, layout, resolution, and color mode.

    ● In the **Label** section, specify the settings such as text, font type, font size, font color, opacity, and text position.

4. If necessary, in the **Layout** section, click the **Edit Layout** button and in the **Picture Package Edit Layout** dialog box, specify the settings such as image layout, size, position, and snap to grid, and click **Save.**

5. In the **Picture Package** dialog box, click **OK** and view the output.

ACTIVITY 8-1
Saving Images for Print

Data Files:

Color Sample Card_Print.psd

Before You Begin:

1. Navigate to the C:\084384Data\Saving Images for Web and Print folder and open the Color Sample Card_Print.psd file.

2. Set the zoom percentage of the document to 10.

Scenario:

You want to present the color sample card you created to your senior officials and colleagues in a print format. Before printing it, you want to ensure that the quality of the output is good. So, you decide to change the settings of the document to get the desired output.

---

1. Change the color mode and verify the image resolution of the color sample card.

    a. Observe that the document tab reflects its current color mode.

    b. Choose **Edit→Convert to Profile.**

    c. In the **Convert to Profile** dialog box, in the **Destination Space** section, verify that in the **Profile** drop-down list, **Working CMYK - U.S. Web Coated (SWOP) v2** is selected.

    d. Click **OK.**

    e. Observe that the document tab reflects the changed color mode.

    f. Choose **Image→Image Size.**

    g. In the **Image Size** dialog box, in the **Document Size** section, in the **Resolution** text box, double-click and type *300*

    h. Click **OK.**

---

2. Save the file in the TIFF format.

    a. Choose **File→Save As** to display the **Save As** dialog box.

    b. From the **Format** drop-down list, select **TIFF (*.TIF;*.TIFF).**

    c. In the **Save Options** section, uncheck the **Alpha Channels** and **Layers** check boxes and then click **Save.**

    d. In the **TIFF Options** dialog box, in the **Image Compression** section, verify that the **NONE** option is selected and click **OK.**

    e. Close the file.

    f. In the **Adobe Photoshop CS5 Extended** message box, click **No.**

OPTIONAL ACTIVITY 8-2
Creating a Picture Package for Print

Data Files:

Logo.psd

Before You Begin:

1. Navigate to the C:\084384Data\Saving Images for Web and Print folder and open the Logo.psd file.

2. Set the zoom percentage of the document to 50.

Scenario:

Your manager is impressed with the logo you created and wants to send it to the client. So, you decide to take printouts of the logo in different sizes on a single sheet because the logo you created will be used by print applications.

1. Create a picture package for printing.

   a. Choose **File→Automate→Picture Package.**

   b. In the **Picture Package** dialog box, in the **Document** section, from the **Layout** drop-down list, select **(2)4x5 (4)2.5x3.5** to change the layout settings.

   c. From the drop-down list to the right of the **Resolution** text box, select **pixels/inch.**

   d. In the **Resolution** text box, verify that **300** is displayed.

   e. From the **Mode** drop-down list, select **CMYK Color.**

   f. Verify that the **Flatten All Layers** check box is checked.

   g. Click **OK.**

2. Save the file in TIFF format.

   a. Observe that the resultant Picture Package file is displayed.

   b. Choose **File→Save As** to display the **Save As** dialog box.

   c. In the **File name** text box, type *My Logo*

   d. From the **Format** drop-down list, select **TIFF (*.TIF;*.TIFF).**

   e. In the **Save Options** section, uncheck the **Layers** check box and click **Save.**

   f. In the **TIFF Options** dialog box, in the **Image Compression** section, verify that **NONE** is selected and click **OK.**

   g. Close the Picture Package file without saving it.

   h. Close the Logo.psd file.

TOPIC B
Save Images for the Web

You saved images for print applications. Now, you want to change the file format of the image to place it on a web page. In this topic, you will save images for the web.

Photoshop helps you create files that are meant for use on web and print applications. You may want to display your personalized design on your web page to get comments from viewers. However, for web applications, you have to save files in suitable formats so that the images do not lose their quality when made available online.

File Formats for the Web

Web graphics are commonly saved in JPEG, PNG, and GIF formats. JPEG images can contain millions of colors and shades, making JPEG the preferred format for photographs. GIF images can contain only 256 colors or shades. However, the quality of the image might be affected if the original image contains more colors. The PNG format is the most robust of all the common web graphic formats. PNG supports up to 48-bit RGB color and 16-bit grayscale. It also supports transparency in images.

Picture Quality Setting

You can specify the quality setting of a JPEG image. When you set a higher quality setting, the resultant image will have a larger file size. A lower quality setting will decrease the image quality and file size.

The Save for Web & Devices Dialog Box

The **Save for Web & Devices** dialog box contains various options that allow you to preview several versions of an image when it is saved using web formats such as GIF, JPEG, and PNG. In addition, you can set options specific to these formats in this dialog box. You can also choose the file format and image quality. Images can be previewed in one of four views: **Original, Optimized, 2-Up,** and **4-Up.** Changing the magnification for one image preview automatically changes it for all four previews.

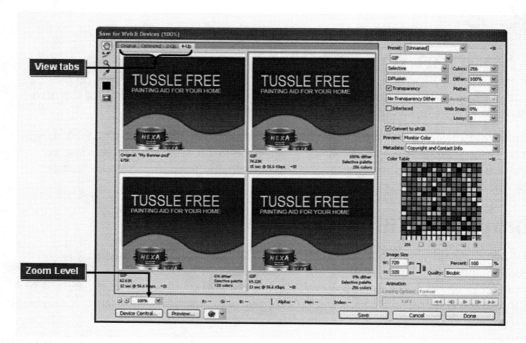

Figure 8-2: *Different previews of an image.*

The Zoomify Export Feature

The **Zoomify Export** feature allows you to include high quality graphic images on the web with zoom controls. These controls will allow web users to zoom in or zoom out the image at specific percentages using the slider control. They can also move to a specific portion in the image by navigating to the left, top, right, or bottom directions using the respective buttons. The **Zoomify™ Export** dialog box can be used to specify the output folder location, the number of image tiles, and the height and width of the image in HTML.

How to Save Images for the Web

Procedure Reference: Save Images in the JPEG Format

To save images in the JPEG format:

1. Choose **File→Save For Web & Devices.**

2. In the **Save For Web & Devices** dialog box, select the desired tab to view images in different versions.

3. Select the desired preview.

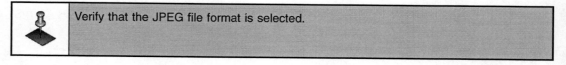

4. Specify the desired optimization options such as quality, blur, and matte for the JPEG format.

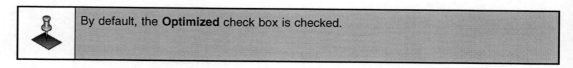

5. In the **Image Size** section, specify the desired size, quality, and resize percentage of the image.

6. Click **Save.**

7. In the **Save Optimized As** dialog box, in the **File Name** text box, specify the desired file name.

8. Click **Save** to save a copy of the file in the JPEG format.

ACTIVITY 8-3
Saving Images for the Web

Data Files:

Color Sample Card_Web.psd

Before You Begin:

1. Navigate to the C:\084384Data\Saving Images for Web and Print folder and open the Color Sample Card_Web.psd file.

2. Set the zoom percentage of the document to 25.

Scenario:

You need to place the color sample card you created on a web page, so that clients can review it. Before doing so, you want to change the resolution of the color sample card, that is ideal for the web. Also, you want to modify the settings of the file such as size, format, and quality to ensure that the images are properly displayed on the web.

---

1. Specify image settings to obtain the best quality.

    a. Choose **File→Save for Web & Devices.**

    b. In the **Save for Web & Devices (100%)** dialog box, select the **2-Up** tab to view the file in different versions.

    c. From the **Zoom Level** drop-down list, select **50%.**

    d. Select the **4-Up** tab to view the file size, quality, and download time of each version.

    e. Select the bottom-left preview tab.

    f. In the right section, from the **Optimized file format** drop-down list, select **JPEG.**

    g. From the **Compression quality** drop-down list, select **Medium.**

    h. In the **Quality** text box, double-click and type *50*

---

2. Specify size settings for the image to optimize it and save the file.

    a. In the **Image Size** section, in the **W** text box, double-click and type *500*

    b. Click **Save.**

    c. In the **Save Optimized As** dialog box, in the **File name** text box, type *Color Sample Card*

    d. Navigate to the C:\084384Data\Saving Images for Web and Print folder.

    e. Click **Save.**

    f. Close the color sample card document without saving the changes.

TOPIC C
Save Images as PDF

You saved images for use in print applications and the web. You may need to send the file to someone who does not have the Photoshop application or you may want to make sure that your design is not tampered with. In this topic, you will save images as PDF.

You may need to send the file to your client or your supervisor for review and feedback. They might not have the Photoshop application or you may want to make sure that the design you have created is not modified by anyone. In such cases, you can avoid rework as Photoshop allows you to save images in the PDF format.

Adobe PDF Presets

PDF presets are groups of settings that are used to create consistent PDF files by balancing file size and quality based on how the files will be used. These presets are available in the **Adobe PDF Presets** dialog box. The following table describes the different PDF preset options.

Preset	Description
High Quality Print	Creates PDF files for printing on desktop printers and proofers. They are compatible with Acrobat and Adobe Reader 5.0 and later.
PDF/X-1a:2001	Creates PDF files that conform to the PDF/X-1a:2001 ISO standards. They are compatible with Acrobat and Adobe Reader 4.0 and later.
PDF/X-3:2002	Creates PDF files that conform to the PDF/X-3:2002 ISO standards. They are compatible with Acrobat and Adobe Reader 4.0 and later.
PDF/X-4:2008	Creates PDF files that conform to the PDF/X-4:2008 ISO standards. They are compatible with Acrobat and Adobe Reader 5.0 and later.
Press Quality	Creates PDF files for high-quality printing. They are compatible with Acrobat and Adobe Reader 5.0 and later.
Smallest File Size	Creates PDF files for use on screen, in email, and on the Internet. They are compatible with Acrobat and Adobe Reader 6.0 and later.

 PDF/X Standard refers to a standard for graphic content exchange defined by the International Organization for Standardization (ISO).

Each PDF preset includes options for modifying the General, Compression, Output, and Security settings.

 For more information about ISO standards for graphic content exchange, refer to the Adobe Acrobat User Guide.

How to Save Images as PDF

Procedure Reference: Open a PDF Document in Photoshop

To open a PDF document in Photoshop:

1. Choose **File→Open,** select the desired PDF document, and click **Open.**
2. In the **Import PDF** dialog box, specify the desired settings.
    -   In the **Select** section, click the thumbnails to select the pages you want to import.
    -   In the **Page Options** section, specify the required settings.
        -   In the **Name** text box, change the title of the PDF document.
        -   From the **Crop To** drop-down list, select an option to specify which part of the document needs to be imported.
    -   In the **Image Size** section, specify the desired settings such as image dimensions, resolution, image mode, and bit depth of an image or document.
3. Click **OK.**

Procedure Reference: Save a PDF Document in Photoshop

To save a PDF document in Photoshop:

1. Choose **File→Save As.**
2. In the **Save As** dialog box, in the **Format** drop-down list, select **Photoshop PDF (*.PDF;*.PDP).**
3. Click **Save.**

Procedure Reference: Place a PDF Document in Photoshop

To place a PDF document in Photoshop:

1. Choose **File→Place.**
2. In the **Place** dialog box, select the PDF document and click **Place.**
3. In the **Place PDF** dialog box, in the **Select** section, select the **Page** or **Image** option, select the desired page or image and click **OK.**
4. Double-click within the transform handles to place the image.

Procedure Reference: Manage PDF Presets

To manage PDF presets:

1. Choose **Edit→Adobe PDF Presets.**
2. In the **Adobe PDF Presets** dialog box, in the **Presets** section, select the desired preset.
3. Click **Done.**

ACTIVITY 8-4
Saving Images as PDF

Data Files:

Color Sample Card_Print.psd

Before You Begin:

Navigate to the C:\084384Data\Saving Images for Web and Print folder and open the Color Sample Card_Print.psd file.

Scenario:

Before finalizing the design, you want to send it to the department head and incorporate any feedback. Because you are not sure whether he has Photoshop installed on his system, you decide to save the file in the PDF format so that it can be viewed and printed.

---

1. Save the design document as PDF for easy viewing of the files.

    a. Choose **File→Save As** to display the **Save As** dialog box.

    b. In the **File name** text box, type *Color Sample Card*

    c. From the **Format** drop-down list, select **Photoshop PDF (*.PDF;*.PDP)** and click **Save.**

    d. In the **Adobe Photoshop CS5 Extended** message box, click **OK.**

    e. In the **Save Adobe PDF** dialog box, in the **Adobe PDF Preset** drop-down list, verify that **[High Quality Print]** is selected.

    f. From the **Compatibility** drop-down list, select **Acrobat 7 (PDF 1.6).**

    g. In the left pane, select **Compression.**

    h. In the **Options** section, in the **for images above** text box, double-click and type *200*

    i. Click **Save PDF.**

    j. In the **Save Adobe PDF** message box, click **Yes.**

    k. Close the Color Sample Card.psd file.

---

2. View the created PDF.

    a. Navigate to the C:\084384Data\Saving Images for Web and Print folder.

    b. Double-click the **Color Sample Card.pdf** file to open it.

    c. Close the PDF file.

    d. Close Windows Explorer.

    e. Choose **File→Exit** to close the Photoshop application.

Lesson 8 Follow-up

In this lesson, you saved an image in different formats so that it could be shared and viewed in other applications, and optimized them for different media. By optimizing images, you can ensure that the best output of the image is obtained for a specific medium.

1. **Give examples of situations in your workplace when you chose specific file formats for different outputs.**

2. **How will you make use of the PDF presets when handling PDF files in Photoshop?**

Follow-up

In this course, you explored the Photoshop CS5 interface and used several tools for selecting parts of images. You moved, duplicated, and resized images. You also learned to use layers and to apply layer effects and filters for creating special effects. Additionally, you used painting tools and blending modes to create shading effects. Finally, you saved images for use in print and web applications.

1.   **How will customizing your Photoshop workspace environment help you?**

2.   **Now that you have worked with the layers feature in Photoshop, how will this affect your work with design and photography?**

3.   **What are the factors that you need to consider while saving images for web and print applications?**

What's Next?

Adobe® Photoshop® CS5: Level 2 is the next course in this series. In this course, you will deal with the advanced features and tools in Photoshop.

A Organizing Assets Using Adobe® Bridge

Lesson Time: 40 minutes

Objectives:

In this lesson, you will manage assets by using the various tools in Adobe® Bridge. This will enable you to organize your files and work more efficiently.

You will:

- Explore the Adobe Bridge workspace.
- Work with Adobe Bridge.
- Work with stacks and filters in Adobe Bridge.
- Apply metadata and keywords to files in Adobe Bridge.
- Create a web gallery.

Introduction

You created images of various file formats using Adobe® Photoshop® CS5. Now, you want to familiarize yourself with the Photoshop file management functionality of Adobe Bridge and use it to manage your assets. In this lesson, you will work with assets using Adobe Bridge.

A well-organized file system is essential for an efficient workflow. It allows you to reorganize your assets and group assets, and locate specific assets. If you understand the functions of Adobe Bridge, you will be able to manage assets efficiently.

This lesson covers all or part of the following Adobe Visual Communication using Photoshop CS5 objectives:

- Topic A
  - Objective 3.4b: Identify techniques used to produce reusable images.

TOPIC A
Explore Adobe Bridge

You created some assets and a document using Photoshop. Now, you need a well-organized file system to manage all your creative assets. Using Adobe Bridge, you can access and locate files easily.

You are a novice user of Adobe Bridge and you want to become familiar with the application. By exploring the workspace, you will be able to use the application efficiently, and access and locate files easily.

Adobe Bridge

Adobe® Bridge is an independent file management system that enables you to manage Adobe and other application files from a central location. Using Adobe Bridge, you can create and manage folders, add and edit metadata and keywords, and search for files. You can also preview, rotate, delete, or move files. In addition, you can preview images as a full screen, slide show, thumbnail, detail, and list, and you can also sort assets in various ways. You can use either the **Go to Bridge** button located on the Application bar or the **Browse in Bridge** command on the **File** menu to launch Adobe Bridge. The interface of the Adobe Bridge can be customized based on specific requirements and can be saved for future use.

Adobe Version Cue and Adobe Stock Photos

Adobe Bridge allows you direct access to both Adobe® Version Cue®, Photoshop's project management feature, and Adobe® Stock Photos, a service that allows you to search, test, and purchase stock images.

Adobe Bridge Workspace

The Adobe Bridge workspace has a number of components that can be used to organize assets.

Component	Description
Menu bar	A bar that contains various Adobe Bridge commands.
CONTENT	A panel that displays content when you select a folder in the **FAVORITES, FOLDERS, FILTERS,** or **COLLECTIONS** panel.
FILTER	A panel that controls files that should appear in the **CONTENT** panel and their associated metadata.
PREVIEW	A panel that allows you to preview and compare images.
FOLDERS	A panel that displays the folder hierarchy and helps you navigate to the desired folder quickly.
FAVORITES	A panel that lists the folders that you visit often. It also provides a link to Adobe Stock Photos, Version Cue, and the home page of Adobe Bridge. You can organize favorites by dragging items that you would like to frequently use from the **FOLDERS** panel to the **FAVORITES** panel.
METADATA	A panel that allows you to add metadata information for the selected files.

Component	Description
KEYWORDS	A panel that allows you to add keyword information for the selected files.
Path Bar	A bar that contains shortcuts of commonly used options in Adobe Bridge. It also contains options that allow you to create and delete a folder, and navigate to different folders.

Views in Adobe Bridge

Adobe Bridge offers several options for viewing files and folders.

View	Enables You To
Full Screen Preview	Preview the selected file in the **CONTENT** panel in full screen view.
Slideshow	Display a slide show of all the items in the **CONTENT** panel.
Slideshow Options	Customize the display of all assets in the slide show, using the different options in the **Slideshow Options** dialog box.
Review Mode	Display the images as thumbnails in the **CONTENT** panel. You can preview each image individually using the navigation buttons in the Review mode.
Compact Mode	Reduce the Bridge to a small window that can be floated like a panel.
As Thumbnails	Display the images in the **CONTENT** panel as a group of thumbnails.
As Details	Display the images along with additional information about the image.
As List	Display the images in the **CONTENT** panel as a list.
Show Thumbnail Only	Display the thumbnail view of the images in the **CONTENT** panel.
Grid Lock	Display the assets in a grid lock view. This view allows you to easily reckon the number of images in the **CONTENT** panel.
Show Reject Files	Display the images that were rejected. Rejected files in Adobe Bridge can be restored, whereas deleted files cannot be recovered.
Show Hidden Files	Display hidden files such as cache files and provisionally removed Version Cue files.
Show Folders	Display folders along with other images.
Show Items from Subfolders	Display images within a subfolder in the **CONTENT** panel.

View	Enables You To
Sort	Select the order in which files are displayed. Files can be sorted in ascending or descending order, or manually.
Refresh	Update the **CONTENT** panel. This is useful for handling Version Cue files that do not update automatically.

The Sort Options

Files can be sorted by specifying the file information such as file name and file size. You can also sort by specifying the dates of document creation and document modification, or by specifying other information such as dimensions, resolution, and color profile.

The View As Options

Adobe Bridge offers several options for viewing the workspace. The default views are Thumbnail and Details. The Details view displays items in a grid, whereas the Thumbnail view displays a list of thumbnails with information about each file.

ACTIVITY A-1
Exploring Adobe Bridge

Before You Begin:

The Adobe Photoshop application should be kept open.

Scenario:

The color sample card has been created but you have the support files in different folders on your local system. Now, you want to manage the assets you used for creating the color sample card using Adobe Bridge. Before you begin with this task, you want to explore Adobe Bridge.

1. Display Adobe Bridge and navigate to the Managing Assets with Adobe Bridge folder.

   a. Choose **File→Browse in Bridge.**

   b. If necessary, in the **Adobe Bridge** message box, click **No.**

   c. Select the **FOLDERS** panel.

   d. In the **FOLDERS** panel, select **Computer** to display its content in the **CONTENT** panel.

   e. In the **CONTENT** panel, double-click **Local Disk (C:)** to display its contents.

   f. In the **CONTENT** panel, double-click the **084384Data** folder to view its contents.

   g. Navigate to the Managing Assets folder.

2. View the files in the **CONTENT** panel.

   a. Choose **View→As Details** to display additional information about the folders.

   b. Double-click the Assets folder.

   c. Scroll down and select the **Paint Can.png** file to preview it in the **PREVIEW** panel.

   d. Choose **View→As List** to list the items in the **CONTENT** panel.

TOPIC B
Work with Adobe Bridge

Though Photoshop allows you to work with files of different formats, it can be a tedious task to organize files, especially if there are many. Managing these files is a lot easier using Adobe Bridge. In this topic, you will work with Adobe Bridge.

While organizing your files, you might have to move them from their current locations to a centralized location. This can be a tedious task if it involves a large number of files. Adobe Bridge provides options that allow you to easily reorganize a large number of files to a centralized location.

The COLLECTIONS Panel

The **COLLECTIONS** panel helps you easily search for files in Adobe Bridge. The **New Collection** button and the **New Smart Collection** button, when clicked, create virtual folders in the panel. These folders perform the search and display the search results in the **CONTENT** panel.

Button	Allows You To
New Collection	Save files in the **CONTENT** panel as a collection. You can easily retrieve the files by just clicking a new collection folder in the panel.
New Smart Collection	Save a search term such as file names, keywords, document type, and so on. The new smart collection, when clicked, performs a search based on the specified criteria.
Delete Collection	Delete a collection.
Edit Smart Collection	Edit a search term such as file names, keywords, document type, and so on.

How to Work with Adobe Bridge

Procedure Reference: Select a Workspace for Adobe Bridge

To select a workspace for Adobe Bridge:

1. Launch the Adobe Bridge application.
    *   In the **Adobe Photoshop CS4 Extended** application window, choose **File→Browse in Bridge.**
    *   Choose **Start→All Programs→Adobe Bridge CS4.**
    *   In the **Adobe Photoshop CS4 Extended** application window, on the Options bar, click the **Launch Bridge** button.
2. Select a workspace for Adobe Bridge using the Adobe Bridge window.
    *   Click **FILMSTRIP** to display thumbnails of files horizontally in the **CONTENT** panel along with a preview of the selected item in the **PREVIEW** panel.
    *   Click **METADATA** to display the metadata information.
    *   Click **ESSENTIALS** to return to the default display.

 You can choose any of the other workspaces available by clicking the workspace buttons at the bottom-right corner of the window.

Procedure Reference: Manage Files in Adobe Bridge

To manage files in Adobe Bridge:

1. Launch the Adobe Bridge application.
2. Navigate to the folder that has the file to be moved.
3. Select the file you want to move.
4. Place files in different locations using Adobe Bridge.
    *   Choose **Edit→Copy** or right-click the file and choose **Copy** to copy files in Adobe Bridge.
    *   Choose **Edit→Cut** or right-click the file and choose **Cut** to cut the file.

 You can also move or copy files by choosing **File→Move to** or **File→Copy to** and then selecting the desired location.

5. Navigate to the desired location and choose **Edit→Paste.**
6. If necessary, rename the file.
    a. Right-click the file and choose **Rename.**
    b. Type the desired name and press **Enter.**
7. If necessary, delete an asset.
    *   Right-click the file and choose **Delete.** In the **Adobe Bridge** message box, click **OK** or;
    *   Choose **File→Delete** and in the **Adobe Bridge** message box, click **OK** or;
    *   Click the **Delete item** button and in the **Adobe Bridge** message box, click **OK.**

Procedure Reference: Save as Smart Collection

To save as smart collection:

1.   Choose **Edit→Find.**
2.   If necessary, from the **Filename** drop-down list, select the desired option.
3.   If necessary, from the **contains** drop-down list, select the desired option.
4.   In the **Find** dialog box, in the **Enter Text** text box, type the desired keyword.
5.   If necessary, from the **Match** drop-down list, select the desired option.
6.   Click **Find.**
7.   In the **Find Criteria** options bar, click the **Save As Smart Collection** icon.
8.   In the **Collections** panel, rename the New Smart Collection folder as desired.
9.   Press **Enter.**

Procedure Reference: Create a Collection

To create a collection:

1.   Choose **Window→Collections Panel.**
2.   In the **COLLECTIONS** panel, navigate to the desired folder where you want to run a search.
3.   At the bottom of the **COLLECTIONS** panel, select the new collection button.
4.   In the **COLLECTIONS** panel, in the **New Collection** text box, type the desired search term.
5.   In the **COLLECTIONS** panel, click the newly created collection to view the files.

Procedure Reference: Create a Smart Collection

To create a smart collection:

1.   Choose **Window→Collections Panel** to display the **Collections** panel.
2.   At the bottom of the **Collections** panel, select the **New Smart Collection** button.
3.   In **Smart Collection** dialog box, specify the search criteria and click **Save.**
4.   In the **COLLECTIONS** panel, in the **New Smart Collection** text box, type the desired name and press **Enter.**
5.   If necessary, in the **COLLECTIONS** panel, click a newly created smart collection to run the search.

ACTIVITY A-2
Working with Adobe Bridge

Before You Begin:

The Adobe Bridge application is open.

Scenario:

The assets that you used to create the color sample card are in different folders on your local system, and you find it difficult to locate them. You want all the assets to be in a specific location that is easily accessible. Before you move the assets to the desired location, you use the Adobe Bridge application to preview certain documents.

1.   Create a folder and move the color sample card into it.

   a.   In Adobe Bridge application window, on the Application bar, click **FILMSTRIP** to display the thumbnails of files horizontally in the **CONTENT** panel along with a preview of the selected item in the **PREVIEW** panel.

   b.   Navigate to the Managing Assets folder.

   c.   At the top-right corner of the **Adobe Bridge** window, click the **Create a new folder** button.

   d.   Type *Brochure Collections* and press **Enter.**

   e.   Select the **Color Sample Card.psd** file.

   f.   Choose **Edit→Cut.**

   g.   Double-click the **Brochure Collections** folder and choose **Edit→Paste.**

2.   Place a copy of the logo into the Brochure Collections folder.

   a.   In the **FOLDERS** panel, expand the **Assets** folder and select the **Logos** subfolder.

   b.   In the **CONTENT** panel, select the **My Brochure.psd** file.

   c.   Choose **Edit→Copy.**

   d.   In the **FOLDERS** panel, select the **Brochure Collections** folder.

   e.   Choose **Edit→Paste.**

3.   View the thumbnails of the assets in the Brochure Collections folder.

   a.   Choose **View→As Details.**

   b.   In the **CONTENT** panel, scroll down and view the details of the file.

TOPIC C

Work with Stacks and Filters in Adobe Bridge

You worked with Adobe Bridge and managed assets by manually rearranging files. The files can be handled easily when they are arranged logically. In this topic, you will use stacks and filters to arrange files.

When there are a number of files to manage, it would become very difficult to locate your files even in a centralized location. Adobe Bridge contains tools that enable you to group your files to easily locate them and list only specific files.

Stacks

Stack is a feature in Adobe Bridge that allows you to group images under a single thumbnail. After grouping the images, you can perform action on multiple files at the same time. When you group more than ten images, the stacks feature allows you to view the files in a sequence from the stack thumbnail.

The FILTER Panel

The **FILTER** panel allows you to filter the list of files to be displayed in the **CONTENT** panel. This panel is displayed at the bottom of the left pane and has components that are arranged as individual sections. The contents of these sections vary based on the current folder selected either in the **FAVORITES** panel or the **FOLDERS** panel. The **FILTER** panel also contains options that allow you to sort data.

The Loupe Tool

The **Loupe** tool allows you to view the magnified portions of an image without actually increasing the image size. It provides a small preview on the image with the magnified display. The **Loupe** tool can be used only within the **PREVIEW** panel of Adobe Bridge.

How to Work with Stacks and Filters in Adobe Bridge

Procedure Reference: Search Using Filters

To search using filters:

1. Launch the Adobe Bridge application.
2. Navigate to the folder where you want to search for the files.
3. If necessary, click the **FILTER** panel.
4. In the **FILTER** panel, select the criteria based on which you want to search.
5. In the **CONTENT** panel, view the results of the search.

Procedure Reference: Create a Stack

To create a stack:

1. Launch the Adobe Bridge application.
2. Select the files you want to stack.
3. Choose **Stacks→Group as Stack.**
4. If necessary, choose **Stacks→Open Stack** to view the stacked files.
5. If necessary, in the **PREVIEW** panel, position the mouse pointer over the file and click at the desired location to have a closer view of the file. Click the image again to hide the **Loupe** tool.

ACTIVITY A-3
Working with Stacks and Filters in Adobe Bridge

Before You Begin:

The Adobe Bridge application is open.

Scenario:

You used a few support files for the creation of the color sample card. You have now been asked to hand off the color sample card along with its support files to the management. The files are in the Assets folder, but you are not sure about the specific location of the files because there are three subfolders. Because there is not much time to locate the files manually, you decide to place the files in the Brochure Collections folder and group them. Also, the preview of the shade card is not explicit.

---

1. Locate the support files that have been used for the color sample card.

    a. On the Application bar, click **ESSENTIALS.**

    b. In the **FOLDERS** panel, select the **Assets** folder.

    c. Choose **View→As Thumbnails.**

    d. In the **CONTENT** panel, observe that all the files in the folders are displayed.

    e. In the **FILTER** panel, expand **File Type** and click **PNG image** to display all the PNG files present in the folders.

---

2. Place the stacked support files in the Brochure Collections folder.

    a. Choose **Edit→Select All.**

    b. Choose **Edit→Cut.**

    c. In the **FOLDERS** panel, select the **Brochure Collections** folder.

    d. Choose **Edit→Paste.**

---

3. Group the support files and stack them.

    a. Select all the paint can images.

    b. Choose **Stacks→Group as Stack.**

    c. In the **CONTENT** panel, observe that all four files have been stacked and appear as a single thumbnail.

    d. Choose **Stacks→Open Stack** to view the stacked files.

---

4. Search for paint can images.

    a. In the **FILTER** panel group, select the **COLLECTIONS** panel.

    b. At the bottom of the **COLLECTIONS** panel, click the **New Smart Collection** button.

---

c. In the **Smart Collection** dialog box, in the **Criteria** section, click in the third text box, type *Paint Can* and click **Save.**

d. In the **CONTENT** panel, observe the **Find Criteria** panel to view the search results.

e. In the **COLLECTIONS** panel, in the **New Smart Collection** text box, type *Paint Cans* and press **Enter.**

TOPIC D
Apply Metadata and Keywords to Files

You used stacks and filters in Adobe Bridge to group and locate files. It is easier to search for files based on their content format or other specific details. In this topic, you will apply metadata and keywords to files.

As you continue to work with a large number of files, it will become increasingly difficult for you to remember the file names. However, you can easily remember the contents of the file. Adobe Bridge allows you to find files based on their content.

Metadata

Metadata is text that describes a file using keywords and other file properties such as the creator, resolution, and color mode among others. In Adobe Bridge, metadata is stored using the eXtensible Metadata Platform, an XML functionality that enables you to share metadata with different Adobe applications. The metadata information can be used to easily locate your files.

Keywords

Definition:

A *keyword* is text that can be assigned to files for identification. The keywords are arranged in categories called keyword sets. A single word or a phrase can be used as a search term to find information on a particular subject. Keywords are often determined based on the characteristic of the search item.

Example:

You have an image of a boy with a puppy sitting in the park, your keywords may include child, boy, puppy, dog, park, as well as others that describe the colors, mood, or use of the image. The image of the purple flowers uses other keywords such as: bouquet, bunch of flowers, close-up, color image, colored background, flower, indoors, nobody, photography, purple, single object, and square. Therefore, these keywords allow you to quickly and efficiently search for an image that meets our original criteria of a bunch of purple flowers.

How to Apply Metadata and Keywords to Files

Procedure Reference: Apply Keywords to Assets in Adobe Bridge

To apply keywords to assets in Adobe Bridge:

1. Launch the Adobe Bridge application.
2. Select the desired file.
3. Select the **KEYWORDS** panel.
4. At the bottom of the **KEYWORDS** panel, click the **New Keyword** button and type the keyword text.
5. Check the newly created keyword to assign it to the file.

Procedure Reference: Apply Metadata to Assets in Adobe Bridge

To apply metadata to assets in Adobe Bridge:

1. Launch the Adobe Bridge application.
2. In the **METADATA** panel, click the pencil icon of the metadata item you want to add or change.
3. Type the text to be added for the metadata item.
4. Click the **Apply** button to add metadata to the file.
5. If necessary, verify if the keywords and metadata are added to the file.
   a. Select the file.
   b. Choose **File→File Info.**
   c. Verify if the keywords are displayed.
   d. From the options list at the top of the dialog box, select the option and verify if the relevant metadata is displayed.

Procedure Reference: Perform a Metadata Search

To perform a metadata search:

1. Choose **Edit→Find.**
2. In the **Find** dialog box, specify the source of the file.
3. Specify the search criteria.
4. From the **Match** drop-down list, select **If Any Criteria Are Met.**
5. Click **Find** to perform a metadata search.

 After performing a metadata search, you can view the information about the file by choosing **File→File Info.**

ACTIVITY A-4
Applying Metadata and Keywords to Files

Before You Begin:

1. The Adobe Bridge application is open.

2. Navigate to the C:\084384Data\Managing Assets\Brochure Collections folder using Adobe Bridge.

Scenario:

The files you used for the color sample card have been organized in a separate folder. In any case, you do not want to waste time by manually searching for the file. You want to be able to easily find the file by searching for specific terms. In addition, you want to include your name as the creator of the color sample card and also the name of your country, so that you will be able to locate the file based on this information.

---

1. Add a few keywords to the Color sample card.

    a. In the **METADATA** panel group, select the **KEYWORDS** panel.

    b. At the bottom-right corner of the **KEYWORDS** panel, click the **New Keyword** button.

    c. Click the **New Keyword** button.

    d. In the highlighted text box, type *Hexa Paints* and press **Enter.**

    e. Check the check box next to the "Paint Can" and "Hexa Paints" keywords.

    f. In the **METADATA** panel, collapse **File Properties** and then expand **IPTC Core** to view the **Keywords** item.

    g. In the **METADATA** panel, collapse **File Properties** and then expand **IPTC Core.**

    h. View the **Keywords** item.

    i. Observe that the keywords have been added.

---

2. Add the name of the creator and the country name to the Color sample card.

    a. In the **METADATA** panel, click the pencil icon next to the **Creator** item.

    b. Type *Tina Morrison*

    c. Click the pencil icon next to the **Creator: Country** item and type *USA*

    d. Click the **Apply** button at the bottom-right corner of the panel.

---

3. Search for the color sample card by specifying the country name.

    a. Choose **Edit→Find.**

    b. In the **Find** dialog box, in the **Criteria** section, in the **Filename** drop-down list, scroll down and select **All Metadata.**

    c. Press **Tab** two times and type *USA*

---

d.   Click the Plus Sign (+) next to the text box.

e.   In the **Criteria** section, in the second row, from the **Filename** drop-down list, select **Keywords.**

f.   Press **Tab** two times and type *Hexa Paints*

g.   Click **Find.**

h.   In the **CONTENT** panel, in the **Find Criteria** section, observe the search results.

---

4.   Verify the keywords in the **File Info** dialog box.

a.   In the **CONTENT** panel, in the **Find Criteria** section, select the first paint can image.

b.   Choose **File→File Info.**

c.   In the **Main Paint Can.png** dialog box, verify that the **Author** and **Keywords** text boxes display the name entered.

d.   At the top left of the dialog box, select the **IPTC** tab.

e.   Verify the **Creator** and **Country** text boxes display the creator and country entered.

f.   Click **OK.**

g.   Click the **Cancel** button to the right of the **New Search** button.

TOPIC E
Create a Web Gallery

You organized files in different formats. There might be a need to publish a set of photos on the web to enable better sharing. In this topic, you will create an online gallery so the photos can be published on the web.

Placing all your photographs on a website is another effective way to make them easily available to family and friends. With Adobe Bridge, you can create galleries that have captions with special effects applied to them, and publish them on the web. Using this option would also save you a lot of time, which otherwise would have been spent on enhancing each photograph.

Web Gallery

Web gallery is a feature that is used to create a web page with thumbnail images and galleries with full size images. When a user clicks the thumbnail image, the image will be displayed in full size as the gallery page. In Adobe Bridge, you can automatically create a web photo gallery by using the Output Module script. Also, it provides a number of templates with one or more style options that can be customized as required.

Additional Plug-ins

Contact sheets, picture packages, and web photo gallery are included as additional plug-ins in Adobe Photoshop CS5. Web photo gallery or web gallery can be accessed through both the Photoshop and Adobe Bridge applications. However, you can use Adobe Bridge to create web galleries effectively. Contact Sheets and Picture Packages can also be accessed through Bridge using the **Photoshop** command on the **Tools** menu.

How to Create a Web Gallery

Procedure Reference: Create a Web Gallery

To create a web photo gallery:

1. Open Adobe Bridge.
    *   Choose **File→Browse in Bridge** or;
    *   At the left corner of the Application bar, click the **Launch Bridge** button or;
    *   Press **Alt+Ctrl+O.**
2. In Adobe Bridge, select the file or folder that contains images that need to be included in the web gallery.
3. Display the **OUTPUT** panel.
    *   Choose **Window→Workspace→Output** or;
    *   On the toolbar, from the workspace switcher drop-down list, select **Output.**
4. In the **OUTPUT** panel, click **WEB GALLERY** and specify the settings.
    *   From the **Template** drop-down list, select an option.
    *   From the **Style** drop-down list, select an option.
5. Click **Refresh Preview** to view the web gallery in the **OUTPUT PREVIEW** panel.
6. Click **Preview in Browser** to view the web gallery in the default web browser.
7. If necessary, specify the settings in the **Site Info, Color Palette, Appearance,** and **Create Gallery** sections to customize the gallery.

ACTIVITY A-5
Creating a Web Gallery

Before You Begin:

Navigate to the C:\084384Data\Managing Assets\Images for Gallery folder in Adobe Bridge to view all images.

Scenario:

You are asked to create a photo gallery with some of the enhanced images and upload it on the official website of the Ristell Paints company.

---

1. Select images for the web gallery.

   a. In Adobe Bridge, choose **Window→Workspace→Output.**

   b. In the **OUTPUT** panel, click **WEB GALLERY.**

   c. Select any file in the **CONTENT** panel.

   d. Choose **Edit→Select All** to select all the images in the **CONTENT** panel.

---

2. Add information about the web gallery.

   a. In the **Site Info** section, in the **Gallery Title** text box, select the text, type *Ristell Paints Photo Gallery* and then press **Tab.**

   b. In the **Gallery Caption** text box, type *Ristell Paints Projects*

   c. In the **Your Name** text box, select the text, type *James Martin* and then press **Tab.**

   d. In the **E-mail Address** text box, type *jamesM@ristellpaints.com*

---

3. Save the web gallery.

   a. In the **OUTPUT** panel, in the **Create Gallery** section, in the **Gallery Name** text box, select the text and type *Ristell Paints Photo Gallery*

    Scroll down to view the **Create Gallery** section.

   b. Click the **Browse** button and in the **Choose a Folder** dialog box, navigate to the C:\084384Data\Managing Assets folder.

   c. Click **OK.**

   d. In the **OUTPUT** panel, click **Save.**

   e. In the **Create Gallery** dialog box, observe the message "Gallery Created" and click **OK.**

---

f.   Close the **Adobe Bridge** window.

4.   Preview the web gallery.

a.   Navigate to the C:\084384Data\Managing Assets\Ristell Paints Photo Gallery folder and open the index.html file.

b.   Click each thumbnail at the left side of the window to view the full size image.

c.   Close the Internet Explorer window.

New Features in Adobe Photoshop CS5

The following table lists the new features pertaining to Adobe® Photoshop® CS5 and where those new features are covered in this course. For example, 1A indicates that the feature is addressed in Lesson 1, Topic A.

Feature	Level	Topic	Activity
The Refine Edge Dialog Box	1	4C	4–5
Content-Aware Fill			
HDR Pro-HDR Merging and HDR Toning Feature			
Adobe Camera Raw 6 Plug-in			
The Mixer Brush – Bristle Tips	1	4C, 6A	6–2
The Puppet Warp tool			
Lens Correction - Adobe Lens Profile Creator			
Adobe Repousse			
16-bit PSD to 8-bit JPG format in single step			
Reversing clone source in CLONE SOURCE panel			
Default values for Shadows/Highlights changed from 50% to 35%	1	7B	
Move a selection when the active layer is hidden	1	4A	
Deleting empty layers			

Feature	Level	Topic	Activity
Straighten button for Ruler tool	1	4A	
Close all open images without saving option	1	4A	
Last folder as default folder for Save As option	1	2B	
Drag and Drop files into Photoshop to create a new layer	1	5A	
Lens Correction filter improvement plus more			
The Lab - Black & White Technique action			
Bridge, runs as a panel in Photoshop	1	2A	
Live Workspaces and customizing the workspace switcher	1	2B	
Custom Panels with Configurator 2.0	1	2B	
Cross-platform 64-bit support			
Adobe CS Live Services	1	2A	

Lesson Labs

Lesson labs are provided as an additional learning resource for this course. The labs may or may not be performed as part of the classroom activities. Your instructor will consider setup issues, classroom timing issues, and instructional needs to determine which labs are appropriate for you to perform, and at what point during the class. If you do not perform the labs in class, your instructor can tell you if you can perform them independently as self-study, and if there are any special setup requirements.

Lesson 1 Lab 1

Understanding Project Plans

Scenario:

You want to ensure that you are familiar with the project definition, scope, and goals of a project. Also, you need to familiarize yourself with factors that need to be considered toward the design and development of the project. You want to test your knowledge of the project and its various factors.

1. **Which guideline should be considered when determining the target audience?**

   a) Analyze only the gender and profession of a target audience.

   b) Content developed for a target audience must be meaningful and relevant.

   c) Understanding client requirements is more important than understanding audience requirements.

   d) Do not use a survey method to determine the target audience.

2. **True or False? A project is a well-defined task that has a beginning and an end, which results in a unique product or service.**

   ___ True

   ___ False

3. **True or False? Copyright terminology applies to any form of work, idea, or information that is substantial and distinctive in any medium and it is important to understand and use copyright terms correctly.**

   ___ True

   ___ False

Lesson 2 Lab 1

Exploring the Adobe Photoshop Interface

Data Files:

Logo.png, enus_084384_02_1_lab.zip

Scenario:

You are a graphic designer in an organization and you need to create a brochure for the Ristell paints company using the Adobe Photoshop CS5 application. Because you are not familiar with the CS5 application, you decide that exploring the application will help you get acquainted with it. Also, you want to remove unnecessary panels that you may not require for your project to make the workspace organized.

1. Launch the Adobe Photoshop CS5 application.

2. Open the Logo.png file from the C:\084384Data\Exploring the Adobe Photoshop Environment folder.

3. Close the **COLOR, SWATCHES, STYLES, ADJUSTMENTS, MASKS, PATHS, MINI BRIDGE,** and **HISTORY** panels.

4. Save the workspace as *My Workspace Environment.*

5. Close the Logo.png file.

Lesson 3 Lab 1

Ascertaining Graphic Type and Resolution

Data Files:

Ristell Logo.eps, Ristell Logo.psd, enus_084384_03_1_lab.zip

Scenario:

You have to create a brochure for Ristell Paints. Before you begin the project, you will to decide on the type of graphics to create your desired final output. You have a set of files that can be used to observe the differences between them, but before that you may want to set measurements for the document per your requirements. After you have observed the differences, you may want to ascertain the size of the image to see if it suits your print requirements.

---

1. Open the Ristell Logo.psd and Ristell Logo.eps files from the C:\084384Data\Determining Graphic Type and Resolution folder and change the document units to pixels.

---

2. Change the size of the image in the Ristell Logo.psd file so that the **Width** measures *280* and observe the differences.

---

3. Save the file as *My Ristell Logo.psd* and close it.

---

4. Close the Ristell Logo.eps file without saving it.

Lesson 4 Lab 1

Working with Selections

Data Files:

Brochure.psd, House.psd, Red Paint Can.png, enus_084384_04_1_lab.zip

Before You Begin:

1. Open the Brochure.psd file from the C:\084384Data\Working with Selections folder and change the measurement units to pixels.

2. Open the House.psd file from the C:\084384Data\Working with Selections folder and change the measurement units to pixels.

3. Open the Red Paint Can.png file from the C:\084384Data\Working with Selections folder and change the measurement units to pixels.

Scenario:

You need to create a brochure using a set of supporting files and the background template of the brochure that has already been created and approved by one of your colleagues. You realize that the color of the background template is solid and can be made natural with a little modification. Also, you feel that the background of the house image is not required because you are going to use the house as an individual object on the brochure.

---

1. In the House.psd file, select the background of the house image using the **Magic Wand** tool.

---

2. Delete the background around the house image and deselect the selection.

---

3. Transfer the home image from the House.psd file to the Brochure.psd file and close the House.psd file without saving it.

---

4. Position the house image so that the bottom-right corner of the image aligns with the bottom-right edge of the background of the brochure.

---

5. Transfer the red paint can image from the Red Paint Can.png file onto the brochure file and place it at the bottom-left corner of the background.

---

6. Set the gradient values for the background of the brochure using the value *ccffff* for the left color stop and *0066cc* for the right color stop.

---

7. Apply the gradient by clicking at the top-left corner of the document and dragging to the roof of the house.

---

8. Save the file as *My Brochure.psd* and close it.

Lesson 5 Lab 1
Manipulating Layers

Data Files:

Brochure.psd, enus_084384_05_1_lab.zip

Before You Begin:

1. Open the Brochure.psd file from the C:\084384Data\Working with Layers folder.
2. Ensure the measurement unit is set to pixels.

Scenario:

You want to organize the layers in your brochure so that you can identify them easily. You also want to add the marketing byline for the brochure and format it so as to enhance its appearance.

---

1. Rename the layer with the home image as *Home* and the layer with the red paint can as *Paint Can.*

---

2. Select the **Horizontal Type** tool and set the font type to **Swiss 911UCm BT,** font size to *63.6 pt,* and font color to *003366.*

---

3. Display the rulers and at the point of intersection of the 200-pixel mark on the horizontal ruler and the 400-pixel mark on the vertical ruler, enter the text *Give Life to your Imagination.* Ensure that the word "Imagination" is placed below the letter "L" of the word "Life."

---

4. Increase the font size of the word "Life" to *92.88 pt* and the word "Imagination" to *95.28 pt.*

---

5. Using the **Transform** command, position the red paint can image at X: *509* and Y: *2977.*

---

6. Select and group all flower layers, rename the group as *Flowers,* and place it below the Home layer.

---

7. Change the **Opacity** of the **Branch** and the **Butterfly** layers to *80%.*

---

8. Save the file as *My Brochure.psd* and close it.

Lesson 6 Lab 1
Painting Images

Data Files:

Brochure.psd, enus_084384_06_1_lab.zip

Before You Begin:

Open the Brochure.psd file from the C:\08434Data\Enhancing Images with Paint and Filters folder and ensure that the measurement unit is in pixels.

Scenario:

You feel that you need to give a dark background for the text given at the bottom of the brochure to make it readable. Also, you need to change the colors of some of the flowers to match the color of the shade card given by Ristell Paints.

1. Add a new layer above the Home layer. Draw a strip using the **Rectangular Marquee** tool over the contact address from the left of the brochure to the right.

2. Apply the *003366* color inside the drawn rectangular strip and deselect the selection.

3. In the **LAYERS** panel, in the Flowers folder, for the Flower 1 layer, apply *e6b8b8* as a fill.

4. Similarly, for the Flower 2 and Flower 3 layers, change the color to *f2d97e* and *8cdcb4* respectively.

5. Save the file as *My Brochure.psd* and close it.

Lesson 7 Lab 1

Applying Color Adjustments

Data Files:

Brochure.psd, enus_084384_07_1_lab.zip

Before You Begin:

1. Open the Brochure.psd file from the C:\084384Data\Exploring Image Modes and Color Adjustments folder.
2. Ensure the measurement unit is set to pixels.

Scenario:

The colors in the Ristell paints shade card are used for the flowers in the brochure. You feel that the colors are not exactly matching with the shade card. You want to adjust the color modes and also want to reduce the size of the document in order to send it for the client's approval.

---

1. Hold down **Ctrl** and click the Flower 1 layer thumbnail. With the **Colorize** option enabled, change the **Hue** to *360,* **Saturation** to *73,* and **Lightness** to *-28* using the commands on the menu.

---

2. Similarly, for the Flower 2 layer, with the **Colorize** option enabled, change the **Hue** to *247,* **Saturation** to *69,* and **Lightness** to *-35* using the commands on the menu.

---

3. For the Flower 3 layer, with the **Colorize** option enabled, change the **Hue** to *124,* **Saturation** to *57,* and **Lightness** to *-14* using the commands on the menu.

---

4. Save the file as *My Brochure Final.psd* and then flatten the image.

---

5. Save and close the file.

Lesson 8 Lab 1

Saving Images for Different Media

Data Files:

Brochure Final.psd, enus_084384_08_1_lab.zip

Before You Begin:

Open the Brochure Final.psd file from the C:\084384Data\Saving Images for Web and Print folder and ensure that the measurement unit is in pixels.

Scenario:

You want to market the brochure you created through different media such as web and print. So, you decide to modify the design suitable for both the web and print and make a copy of the design in different formats that will best support the output.

---

1. Change the color mode to CMYK and the resolution to *350* for the brochure.

---

2. Save the brochure as a copy in the TIFF format with the title *My Brochure_Print.*

---

3. Save the Brochure Final.psd file as a copy in the JPEG format with the default settings and name it *My Brochure_Web.*

---

4. Similarly, save the Brochure Final.psd file as a copy in the PDF format and name it *My Brochure_PDF.* Set the compatibility to Acrobat 7 or above.

---

5. Close the file and close the Photoshop application.

Solutions

Lesson 1

Activity 1-1

1. **What are the factors that need to be considered while planning a project? (Choose three.)**

   ✓ a) Design elements

      b) Geographical location where the project will be implemented

   ✓ c) Target audience

   ✓ d) Final output

2. **True or False? Scope definitions are shaped by deliverables, assumptions, and constraints that are documented during project initiation.**

   ✓ True

   __ False

Activity 1-2

1. **You want to add a copyright statement to a website before publishing it. What statement elements are appropriate?**

   ✓ a) The copyright symbol (©)

      b) The state of origin

   ✓ c) The copyholder's name

   ✓ d) The word "Copyright"

   ✓ e) The statement "All rights reserved"

2. **While browsing images on the web, you come across an image that would be per-fect for a web page you are working on. What action will you take to use the image?**

    a) Enlarge the image and copy it to your local system.

    b) Copy the image and make very slight changes so it is not like the original image.

    ✓ c) Check for copyright information and then contact the designer for permission.

    d) Check for copyright information, and if it is not evident, copy and use the image.

Lesson 1 Follow-up

Lesson 1 Lab 1

1. **Which guideline should be considered when determining the target audience?**

    a) Analyze only the gender and profession of a target audience.

    ✓ b) Content developed for a target audience must be meaningful and relevant.

    c) Understanding client requirements is more important than understanding audience requirements.

    d) Do not use a survey method to determine the target audience.

2. **True or False? A project is a well-defined task that has a beginning and an end, which results in a unique product or service.**

    ✓ True

    ___ False

3. **True or False? Copyright terminology applies to any form of work, idea, or informa-tion that is substantial and distinctive in any medium and it is important to understand and use copyright terms correctly.**

    ✓ True

    ___ False

Lesson 3

Activity 3-1

1. **True or False? Vector graphics are composed of mathematically defined shapes.**

    ✓ True

    ___ False

2. **True or False? Raster graphics require less memory and storage to manipulate them.**

    ___ True

    ✓ False

3. **Which statements about raster graphics are true?**

   ✓ a) Raster graphics are composed of a grid of pixels.

      b) Raster graphics are composed of lines defined by a set of mathematical instructions.

   ✓ c) Raster graphics can be created using the Photoshop application.

      d) Raster graphics are composed of curves and geometrical shapes.

Activity 3-2

3. **True or False? A greater ppi results in higher resolution and quality but smaller file size.**

   __ True

   ✓ False

Lesson 4

Activity 4-3

2. **Which statement is correct with regard to the CHANNELS panel options menu?**

      a) You can create, delete, split, and merge channels but cannot duplicate channels using the CHANNELS panel options menu.

      b) You can create, duplicate, delete, split, and merge channels, but cannot change the size of the thumbnails using the CHANNELS panel options menu.

   ✓ c) You can create, duplicate, delete, split, and merge channels, and change the size of the thumbnails using the CHANNELS panel options menu.

      d) You cannot change the size of the thumbnails using the CHANNELS panel options menu.

Lesson 7

Activity 7-1

1. **Which image does not contain any gray level?**

      a) PNG

      b) JPEG

   ✓ c) BMP

      d) GIF

2. **True or False? Duotone is a 1-channel, 8-bit image.**

   ✓ True

   __ False

Glossary

Adobe® Bridge
A file management system that is independent of any application and lets you manage Adobe and other application files from a central location.

anti-aliasing
A feature that enables you to smoothen jagged edges by placing light pixels around the outside of a selected object.

bitmap
A collection of bits made up of pixels on grids.

blending modes
Options that determine which pixels blend with each other to create a special effect.

BMP
(Bitmap) A graphic image defined by grids composed of pixels.

citations
A quotation showing a word or phrase in reference to a context.

color mode
The mode that is based on color models used for displaying and printing images.

duotone
A type of image that is created by overlaying a color such as blue or red on a grayscale image.

EPS
(Encapsulated PostScript) Used for saving files that are used in print applications.

fill
A property applied to a shape, path, layer or a selection.

filter
A feature that allows you to change the appearance of images by applying special effects.

flattening
A process that merges all the layers of images in the document with the background layer.

gradient
A blend of two or more colors.

grayscale
A black and white digital image composed exclusively of shades of gray varying from black at the weakest intensity and white at the strongest.

guide
A line that helps align objects on the workspace.

HISTORY panel
A panel that allows undoing and redoing actions.

image resolution
The amount of data stored in an image file.

JPG

(Joint Photographic Experts Group) An image file format that supports millions of colors and is highly effective for compressing complex images such as photographs.

kerning

The process of adjusting the space between characters of text.

keyword

Text that is assigned to files for identification.

LAYERS panel

A panel that contains a list of layers, layer groups, and layer effects that are used in a document.

layers

Transparent pieces of an image that are stacked in a document.

Magic Wand tool

A tool that is used to select image areas based on specified color and brightness range.

metadata

Text that describes a file using keywords and other file properties.

opacity

The amount or percentage of transparency within a layer.

pattern

A texture that creates a repetitive or tiled effect.

PDF presets

A group of options used to create consistent PDF files for quality printing.

PDF

(Portable Document Format) A type of file created by Adobe Acrobat that is readable across a wide array of computer platforms.

pixel depth

Data that describes the color of each pixel in a digital image.

pixel dimension

Horizontal and vertical measurements of an image that is usually measured in pixels.

pixels

The smallest unit of a digital image.

ppi

A measure of the number of pixels displayed in an image.

project

A well-defined task based on a particular structure toward achieving a goal.

Quick Selection tool

Allows you to select complex shapes accurately along the defined edges of an image by using an adjustable brush.

raster graphics

Graphics that are composed of a grid, or raster, of small squares called pixels.

scope creep

Change in the scope of a project after commencement of the project.

scope

Refers to the sum total of all products and its features.

stack

A feature of grouping images under a single thumbnail in Adobe Bridge.

SVG

(Scalable Vector Graphics) A vector graphics formatted specifically for web use.

TIFF

(Tagged Image File Format) Used for saving files that are used in print applications.

transform

The scaling, rotating, distorting, shearing, or perspective effects applied to an image or selected areas in an image.

Type layer

A layer that contains editable text to which you can apply the desired formatting.

vector graphics

Graphics that are defined by a set of mathematical instructions.

workspace presets

A collection of predefined workspaces that are
needed to perform specific tasks.

Index